汉英对照

吴希军 著

上海文艺出版社
Shanghai Literature & Art Publishing House

图书在版编目（CIP）数据

致远方 ： 汉英对照 / 吴希军著. -- 上海 ： 上海文艺出版社, 2025. -- ISBN 978-7-5321-9251-9

Ⅰ. I227; I207.22-53

中国国家版本馆CIP数据核字第2025PP8847号

发 行 人：毕　胜
策 划 人：杨　婷
责任编辑：李　平　程方洁
整体设计：建明文化
策划出版：北京泥流文化传媒有限公司

书　　名：致远方
作　　者：吴希军
出　　版：上海世纪出版集团　上海文艺出版社
地　　址：上海市闵行区号景路159弄A座2楼 201101
发　　行：上海文艺出版社发行中心
上海市闵行区号景路159弄A座2楼 201101 www.ewen.co
印　　刷：三河市华东印刷有限公司
开　　本：880×1230 1/32
印　　张：11.375
字　　数：72,000
印　　次：2025年6月第1版 2025年6月第1次印刷
I S B N：978-7-5321-9251-9/I.7257
定　　价：58.00元
告 读 者：如发现本书由质量问题请与印刷厂质量科联系　T：18611130373

吴希军

笔名它乡人、pywxj、无言、柯言等。毕业于郑州大学中文系。作品散见于《工人日报》《河南日报》《郑州大学学报》《濮阳日报》《安阳文艺》等，曾参与多本书籍的编辑编撰工作。

诗之梦（代序）

吴希军

1973年的夏天，两辆大型公共汽车披着标语、挂着红花，载着70多个不满20岁的男女青年，来到内黄县田氏公社——知识青年上山下乡，从学校踏入农村这个广阔天地。从此，我们这些来自内黄县的知青就在田氏农场这个长不到两公里、宽不到一公里的天地里，开始了人生的寻梦。我的诗人梦，大概也是从那里开始的。

这个以一辆拖拉机、两辆马车和几匹骡马为主要生产工具的“家”，隶属于内黄县农业局，由于人员以知识青年为主，所以县知青办公室拨款为我们盖起了十几间宿舍，加上原来的老房子，共有20多间房屋。农场主要任务是培育农作物的优良种子，所以取名“良种繁育场”。为了便于生产和管理，农场建立了由5名支委组成的共青团支部和三个团小组，建立了男生生产排和女生生产排，并成立了科研小组、果园小组、蔬菜小组等。在团支部的基础上，建立了由农场场长、会计、带队干部、农场工人生产队队长等共11人组成的临时领导班子。团支部三位书记中，两人负责领导男生排和女生排的生产，我分工负责宣传学习和团支部的日常工作。知青农场的宣传工作，主要是办墙报，逢年过节要出专刊，重大活动要出专刊，有时学习心得体会也要交流宣传，可以说办墙报成了知青文化生活和学习中的一个重要项目。这应该是我诗人梦的前奏。

一间不到10平方米的简陋红瓦房，是我和3个知青兄弟的“窝”。那三位，一位是笔杆子，一位是美术爱好者，另一位则腿脚勤快；而我在高中毕业时语文考了年级的最高分96分。四个人，一个负责墙报总体和审稿，一个负责有分量的文章，一个负责插图和美术字，一个负责打糨糊和张贴。一时间墙报倒也调动了全场知青们的学习和生活的热情，大家白天下地劳动，收工回来翻翻书、动动笔，也因此无暇参与知青中普遍存在的一些不良爱好。有时为了营造节日气氛，大家更是共同努力去办好壁报，甚至通宵达旦。我们宿舍的几个人、男女排的70多个知青们、甚至全农场的人，还真把这个事当回事了，场长和带队干部有时还给我们几天时间，让我们专心办壁报。毕竟是一群知识青年，我们的壁报后来还办到了县城，代替了农业局的壁报。再后来，在艺术性、知识性和趣味性等方面，除了县文化馆的壁报，其他单位的壁报，只能对我们知青的壁报望“壁”兴叹了，特别是诗歌方面，连县文化馆也要向我们要稿件了。这也许是我被评为安阳地区优秀知青代表的原因之一吧。

办壁报，补白是经常需要的，这迫使我不时地诌几句诗歌，填补和丰富版面，但是真正勾起我的诗人梦的，是1974年下半年发生的一件事。一天，我们知青的带队干部拿来了份文件，原来是河南人民出版社和共青团河南省委要联合出版一本知识青年诗歌集，开始在知青中征稿，领导希望我们应征。我马上将这个精神在全体团员和青年中进行了传达。大家立刻沸腾了，纷纷将自已的得意之作挑选、整理、修改后，交了上去。经过几个月的等待和期盼，在我们就要彻底失望之时，刊用通知书终于来到了。毕竟是全省征稿，我们只有两位知青、三篇诗稿入选，但这也已经是全场的大喜事了，大家纷纷要求入选的作者请客。这是我第一次发表诗歌作品，激动和喜悦的心情是可想而知的。同时，共青团河南省委宣传部还给我来了一封信，大意是认为我的写作有功底，希望再写一首有激情、正面的诗歌，放在诗集的第一部分，要求在元月10日前寄到团省委。这封信是1974年12月29日写的，我收到时离交稿截止期只有三四天了，这可真是名副其实的“时间紧、任务重”。情急之下我想到了我中学的语文老师，想请他帮我。于是，我向老场长说明了情况并请了两天假，立即动身往县城。老师看了信后鼓励我要有信心和决心，完成这个重任，并和我一起构思和修改诗稿，一起讨论和斟酌词句。经过两天的努力，我终于在元月10日前将诗稿寄出。但是，当11月这本收录了50首诗歌、取名《广阔天地新一代》的诗集出版后，我发现那篇费了九牛二虎之力的《上山下乡颂》不在其中。不知是不符合要求，还是寄迟了，或是没有收到，由于没有和团省委宣传部联系，所以至今仍是个谜，也是我寻诗梦中的一个遗憾。

青年是天然的梦想者。既然做起了诗的梦，也就不难理解后来选择高校时，毅然决然放弃了某著名外语学院，选择本省某大学中文系的举动了；也就有了在校刊上发表的《奴才的春天》的诗评；也就有了大学毕业时，我写的被《河南日报》用近半个版予以发表《新诗要向民歌学习》的文章；也就有了同学、师长和家乡县委宣传部门的青睐。一时间，似乎诗人的桂冠就戴在头上，似乎诗的光环就要将我包围。然而世事难料，打破我诗人梦的是毕业分配和现实的工作。

由于工作和生活现实的需要，我被阴差阳错地安排到财税部门，在办公室负责文字材料工作。开始，我还想着能继续圆我的诗人梦，曾应邀参与了《安阳文艺》创刊号和随后几期的诗歌方面的编辑与撰稿工作，曾在业余时间搞些创作和理论探讨，也曾被中国作家协会河南分会青年诗歌学会吸收为会员，但终于在领导的“干啥要吆喝啥”，不能不务正业的批评和规劝下，在调到文化部门无望的迫使下，放弃了诗人梦，只好到什么山上唱什么歌了，踏踏实实干起了税收。虽然，后来在我主编《濮阳税务》季刊时，诗梦也曾死灰复燃，但毕竟旧梦难圆。朋友们扼腕戏谑：呜呼，文坛少了一个诗人，税苑多了一个庸人。

弹指三十余年过去，回首往事，良多感慨。有时曾异想天开，想到将来退休后能否重拾诗的梦。但是岁月无情，因为诗是属于青春的，诗是属于生活的，没有了这些，只能是痴人说梦。也许诗歌——那是我心中永远的女神，是我心中永远的梦。

（原载《枣乡知青》，有删改）

目　录
Contents

辑一　旧体诗
Section I Ancient—Style Poetry

辑二　现代诗
Section II　Modern Poetry

辑三　评　论

Section III　Comment

辑一
Section I

旧体诗
Ancient—Style Poetry

Section I

答友人

诗书一封情谊深，
慰我哀哀欲裂心。
陵园追悼感君往，
通犀只有故时人。
昔日童贞嗟可叹，
今朝秦晋宜自珍。
莫道膝叙无他日，
洹畔相逢话仇恩。

A Poem to a Friend

A letter of poem showing our deep friendship,
Which offers comfort to my heart—wrenching sorrow.
Mourning in the cemetery and remembering the past,
Only old friends can have a spiritual connection in hearts.
Our pure friendship in the past was lamentable,
While friendship today must be valued by myself.
Do not say that there will be no other days for face—to—face communication,
Meeting by the Huan River brings enmity and kindness together.

雄　鸡

歌喉虽已破，
尤作晓前啼。
天下白复夜，
振翅难有力。
儿女成群散，
孤影壁下立。
鸡老雄心在，
不惧毛羽稀。

A Rooster

Although the singing voice is broken,
I still make crow before dawn.
The nights follows days,
It is difficult to flap my wings vigorously.
Children are scattering in groups,
My solitary shadow stands below the wall.
The ambition of me, the old rooster, is still alive,
I am not afraid of sparse feathers.

山　行

花愈掩路径，
人且画中行。
山空芳气新，
鸟鸣传悠情。

Mountain Trip

Lots of flowers almost covering the path,
It seems as if people were moving in a painting.
The empty mountain with fragrant and fresh air,
In which the chirps of birds convey melodious emotions.

心　情

情在心中情无恙，

心在情中心有涯。

是痛是爱情知道，

亦悲亦欢心无他。

失去方知情难寄，

拥有才觉心为家。

唯愿有情皆眷属，

不坠南柯梦中花。

Feeling

Feeling in heart is safe and sound,

While heart is in feeling and has its limits.

Pain, feeling knows or love,

Both sadness and joy belong to it.

Losing it, makes feeling nowhere to go,

Only by possessing it, does the heart find the home.

May all the lovers get married,

Do not fall into the flower of Nanke's dream.

探亲记

南雁返北程，
一飞一声鸣。
父友皆仙去，
吾辈尤探亲。

去城三五里，
盐碱小荒村。
幼时识其路，
不必引路人。

日暮方起身，
安步当车行。
左转复右转，
难辨西和东。

徙步复徙步，
旧路皆不通。
不知村何在，
城郊变城中。

夜幕渐覆盖，
难达亲友庭。
周身汗已出，
心中似有惊。

有心问路人，
怕骗钱财空。
欲拨 110，
又恐扰邻众。

无奈电好友，
开车接回程。
商议昼再寻，
不觉已鼾声。

天亮寻村位，
再问逝者名。
村民惶大悟，
连连指路径。

到得亲戚家，

已无旧时形。
土墙换砖瓦，
陋屋变楼层。

昔我离去时，
哥嫂刚成婚，
今日再来探，
儿孙已成群。

谈起父辈谊，
抗战结深情。
又叙古今事，
热泪眼中涌。

相约再相聚，
依依不舍情。
纵有千万语，
皆在别离中。

北雁复南飞，
一飞一嘶鸣。

清风送日月，

期待春又生。

A Visit to Relatives

The southern geese return to the north,
Flying and honking.
Father and friends already passed away,
Still we visit our relatives.

Three or five miles away from the city,
That is the small barren village of salt alkali.
Since childhood, I know the path.
No need to be guided.

Set off at dusk,
Walk instead of driving.
Turn left and right,
It is difficult to distinguish the directions.

Step by step,
The roads in mind are all blocked.
Without knowing where the village is,
For suburbs have been changed into the city center.

Darkness falls gradually comes,
We are still looking for the graves of our relatives and friends.
I am in a sweat,
There seems to be a shock in my heart.

Though wanting to ask for directions,
We are afraid of being cheated.
To dial 110,
We are afraid of disturbing the neighbors.

Call to my friend out of helplessly,
Then drive us back.
Deliberate to search again the next day,
Unconsciously snoring.

At dawn, searching for the location of village,
Ask the name of the deceased again.
Surprised and enlightened,
The villagers point out the path to us at once.

Arriving at our relatives' homes,
The old looks are no longer present.
The earthen walls are replaced with bricks and tiles,
The humble house has been changed to a beautiful building.

When I left in the past,
My brother and sister—in—law just got married.
Visiting again today,

They have children and grandchildren.

We talked about the elder generation,
Who made deep friendship during the War of Resistance against Japanese Aggression.
We talked about the past and present,
Tears welling up in eyes.

Parted with relutance,
We made an appointment to have a reunion.
Although we had thousands of words,
All hidden in the midst of separation.

The northern geese fly back to the south,
Flying and honking.
The gentle breeze sends the sun and moon,
Looking forward to spring coming again.

仲　春

细雨无声芳草绿，
春风有意桃花红。
最是一年起兴时，
何处不逢诗画情。

Midspring

Drizzle makes the grass green silently.
The spring breeze makes the peach blossoms red.
It is the beginning of the year,
There is poetry and painting everywhere.

春节献诗

爆竹一声天地新，
万紫千红争报春。
九州欢乐传天外，
时代列车又前进。

Dedicating Poetry for the Spring Festival

With the sound of firecrackers, a new year comes,
A myriad of colors competes to be the messenger of spring.
Joy throughout the nation spreads beyond the sky,
The era train is moving forward again.

春　意

朔风狂舞漫天浑，
万里山河万里银。
天公允我有新意，
先露枝头第一春。

Spring

The north wind dances wildly in the sky,
And thousands of miles of mountains and rivers are like covered with silver.
Heaven allows me to make a change,
To be the first exposure of branches in spring.

无　题

风舞瑞雪纷纷下，
疑似神女散天花，
喜看今日梅含苞，
指待来年放光华！

Untitled

The wind dances and the snow falls,
As if a goddess scattering blossoms,
Happy to see the plum blossoms in bud,
Hoping for the full bloom in the coming year!

怀 友

一声鸿雁送夏去，
几叶残荷知秋深。
问候无言遥相忆，
平安冷暖可在心?

Missing a Friend

A honk of goose bade farewell to summer,
A few leaves of wilted lotuses show the late autumn is at the corner.
Greetings of missing to my friend far away are wordless,
Are peace and warmth in your heart?

锅炉叹

朔风吹雪已严冬，
屋内棉衣裹三层。
无语锅炉又背锅，
唯闻年年道歉声。

Sigh of the Boiler

The north wind blows the snow and it's already the harsh winter,
People inside the house are wrapped in three layers of cotton clothes.
The speechless boiler carries a pot once again,
Apologies are heard every year.

寄　远

青山不墨千秋画，
碧水长流万年诗。
若得翠竹磐石意，
何惧两地长相依。

To the Long—distance Relationship

The green mountains look like an immortal painting unfading,
The clear water flows for thousands of years like poetry.
If one gains the spirit of green bamboos tough like rocks,
He would not be afraid of living apart from his lover in the heart.

辞故人

清风伴我天涯去，

明月随君故乡还。

此别关山千万重，

共剪窗烛知何年。

A Farewell to an Old Friend

The gentle breeze accompanies me to the end of the world,

The bright moon follows you back to your hometown.

After this farewell, there will be thousands of mountains between us,

Without knowing when we can meet each other once more.

祝酒令（二首）

其　一

天新地新气象新，
每逢佳节倍思亲。
幸福不忘昔日苦，
安乐尤敬前辈人。

其　二

请君举盏庆新天，
敢将话题指当年。
此别不知几时聚，
何妨一醉如再见。

Toasts (Two Poems)

No.1

The sky and the earth are new, so is the atmosphere,
During holidays, I miss my families even more.
When in happiness, never forget the hardships in the past,
When in peace and joy, please toast to our predecessors.

No.2

Please raise the cup to celebrate the new day,
Dare to mention the topics of the past years.
Without knowing when we'll get together after this farewell,
Why not get drunk as if we met again?

春　心

风传花信雨濯尘，
人随春好春宜人。
草长莺飞今又是，
心潮难掩思君云。

Spring Heart

The wind spreads the message from the flowers, the rain washes away the dust,
People feel comfortable in such a pleasant spring.
Today, again the grass grows and the warblers fly,
It is difficult to hide the surging emotions in my heart because of missing you.

冬至有感

天自今日寒，

夜从明朝短。

漫道风雪狂，

却话丰收年。

Feelings at the Day of Winter Solstice

The weather will get colder from today,

The night will become shorter since the next morning.

Fierce wind and snow are outside,

While a bountiful year is talked about coming at the corner.

岁 末

朔风卷叶飞似蝶，
阳光耀窗瀑如金。
诗书有约恐日短，
笔墨声中又精神。

End of the Year

The north wind blows the leaves which fly like butterflies,
The sunlight shines through the window like a golden waterfall.
Reading books in the daytime and being afraid the day is short,
I get refreshed in writing.

医道吟

叶自飘零花自落，
天人自然共蹉跎。
幸有神农尝百草，
杏林深处有新果。

Chant of Medicine

Naturally, leaves drift and flowers fall,
Nature and humankind walk together.
Thanks to Shennong's tasting a hundred herbs.
There are new fruits deep in the apricot forest.

除　夕

亲友翩翩盈庭门，
灯红酒绿消黄昏。
到底还是故乡好，
烟花丛中又新春。

Chinese New Year's Eve

Relatives and friends visit me all together,
We drink wine and enjoy happy hours until dusk.
After all, I feel my hometown is the best place,
During the fireworks time, a new spring is coming.

春 咏

昨夜风雪九州白，

今日杨柳着绿来。

天公喜施满天银，

地母怒将众花开。

崇山峻岭披新绣，

江河湖海绘锦彩。

冬夏与秋共辑手，

荐尔岁岁首登台。

Spring Ode

Last night's snow whitened everything,

While today, the willows are turning green.

The Heaven God scatters silver everywhere joyfully,

The Heaven God earth orders all flowers to bloom angrily.

Steep mountains and ridges are covered with newly—embroidered clothes,

Rivers, lakes, and seas are painted with colors.

Winter, summer, and autumn fold hands together,

Recommending you to be the first one to start a new year.

他乡人

故土不可见，

亲友岁愈稀。

少年欺日月，

老骥惜伏枥。

In a Strange Land

The homeland is not visible,

Relatives and friends are getting older and older.

Young people do not know cherishing the time.

Old people may still try to achieve the ambition.

画像（二首）

其　一

三教九流尽来往，
吃喝玩乐当书堂。
皆因父辈居高官，
花花公子世无双。

其　二

貌似爽直笑哈哈，
黑豆眼里藏奸诈。
小恩小惠收人意，
只为利己私心大。

Portraits (Two Poems)

No.1

They interact with all sorts of people,
Regard eating, drinking and playing as daily routine.
All because their fathers are high officials,
Playboys are unparalleled in their generation.

No.2

One seems to have a straightforward smile,
While black—beaned eyes are full of deceit.
Small favors winning the hearts and minds,
Just to satisfy their own big self—interest.

七 夕

一年唯一聚，

七夕难七夕。

但得长恩爱，

不悔破戒律。

The Qixi Festival

Gather one time every year,

For it is difficult to realize the meaning of this festival, love and stay together.

For the sake of love,

Breaking the rules with no regrets.

时 光

指缝太宽时光瘦，

转身之际夏成秋。

雪冬脚步料难远，

念春情思不须愁。

Time

Time is too thin,quietly slip through the fingers,
Just for the moment of turning, summer becomes autumn.
The footsteps of snow and winter must be closer,
Do not worry about the arrival of spring.

诗 学

少小学诗苦思忖，
及长写诗方用心。
当年难释诗中意，
再吟已是诗中人。

Poetry

I could not understand the meaning when learning poetry at a young age,
And be careful considering when getting older.
In the past it was difficult to get the meaning of poetry,
While now I become a person in it when reciting again.

夏 夜

——夜大热，难寐，于朦胧中得句。

凉风何处隐?
夜半蝉鸣甚。
辗转似入睡，
热汗已遍身。

Summer Night

——The night is too hot to sleep,
and I get the poem in half—awake.

Where does the cool breeze hide?
Cicadas chirp more loudly in the midnight.
When toss around and be nearly falling asleep,
I'm covered with sweat.

立　冬

时光无声悄然去，

日月有痕往复来。

又是一年朔风季，

且凭杯茶抒胸怀。

Beginning of Winter

Time passes silently,

The sun and moon move back and forth with traces.

It's another year of north wind season.

I express my mind when drinking a cup of tea.

国庆短歌（二首）

其　一

钢水一泄似长江，
稻菽万顷动地香。
大干热汗甩上天，
化作国庆礼花放。

其　二

心中有诗笔难作，
神州辉煌口难说。
国庆礼炮引胸开，
张嘴吐出歌的河。

Short Songs of National Day (Two Poems)

No.1

The molten steel flows like the Yangtze River,
The fragrance of rice and beans comes from ten thousand hectares.
The hot sweat of hard working has flung to the sky,
Becoming fireworks for National Day

No.2

Poetry is in my heart while difficult to be written down,
The glory of China is hard to say.
The National Day salute cannons unlocked the inspiration,
Mouth opens and spits out the river of songs.

告 别

金戈铁马倏忽去，
闲云野鹤悠然来。
纵似背井离乡意，
亦应挥手拂尘埃。

Farewell

Shining spears and armoured horses swiftly go,
Idle clouds and wild cranes leisurely come.
As if leaving hometown behind,
Also should wave your hand to brush the dust.

茶 吟

一缕沁香天上来，

三日劳烦云霄外。

壶中若有春光意，

杯里诗花次第开。

Tea Chant

A wisp of fragrant with scents from the air,

Three days of toil is disapeared.

If there were spring in the pot,

Poetry and flowers would bloom in the cup one after another.

赠同窗

自然规律似水流，
勿喜勿悲亦勿忧。
但得日月开心过，
管他明年几春秋。

To Classmates

The laws of nature are like water flow,
We should keep inner peace with no joy, no sorrow,
and no worry.
Living happily day and night at present,
No matter what will happen next.

秋 到

爽风戏柳微微摇，

残叶无聊片片飘。

娇花应是闭容时，

候雁失声报秋到。

The Arrival of Autumn

The cool breeze sways the willows slightly,

The dry leaves drift in boredom.

Tender flowers have faded,

Geese honk to announce the arrival of autumn.

久雨望晴

阴雨绵绵令人愁，

隔窗仰望浓云头。

欲问茫茫苍天公，

碧空红日几时有?

Hope for Sunny Days After Long—time Raing

The endless rain makes people feel depressed.

Looking up at the thick clouds through the window,

I want to ask the boundless heaven,

When will there be sunny with blue sky and red sun?

寻

空谷寻兰有鸟鸣，

挥汗涉溪无清风。

但得一簇奉堂上，

便胜彩云飘碧空。

Search

Searching for orchids in the empty valley and hearing birds chirping,

Sweat and wade through the stream without breeze.

If only one orchid is found and placed in the hall,

It is better than colorful clouds floating in the blue sky.

赠友人

雾里看花花更萌，
梦中幽思思愈浓。
莫道鸿雁能传书，
难比相聚一刻钟。

To a friend

Looking at flowers in the mist makes them even cuter,
Thinking deeply in the dream makes thoughts grow stronger.
Although the swan goose can transmit letters,
It's incomparable to gather together for a while.

品　茗

静水流深觉三味，

点滴雅俗皆在心。

世上岁月悠悠过，

梦里风尘细细品。

Taste Tea

Still waters run deep which helps people get the true meaning of things,

Every bit of elegance and vulgarity is in the heart.

Time flies by,

Taste the wind and dust in the dream.

农 家

柳絮随风入农家，
便引乡情话桑麻。
酒香语暖意难尽，
相约明年品新茶。

Farmhouse

Willow catkins fly with the wind into the farmhouse,
And people talk about the life in the countryside.
Wine is fragrant, words are warm, and emotions can not be fully expressed,
People make an appointment to taste new tea next year.

冬 雨

大雪时节雨纷纷，
冬至南来风阵阵。
农夫心头布霾雾，
芒种能否遍地金。

Winter Rain

In Major Snow, it rains heavily,
In Winter Solstice, it blows a lot, especially the wind from the south.
The farmer's heart is shrouded in haze and mist,
Whether there will be a harvest in Autumnal Equinox.

叹　秋

雨来不知夏已去，
风起方觉始到秋。
白驹过隙沧桑叹，
红颜易失今日忧。

Sighing of Autumn

When it rains, I do not know that summer has already passed.
When the wind blows, I start to feel the beginning of autumn.
What a pity, time flies like a white horse gaping through a crevice,
Just as beauty fades like a flower.

感 怀

中秋明月光，
友人在远方。
他日我若去，
几人来悲伤?

Reflection

The moon is bright on the Mid—Autumn Festival,
Friends are far away.
If I pass away someday,
How many people would feel sad for me?

忘忧草

晓月破雾马蹄疾，
晚风拂柳笛声残。
自古边关多风雨，
平安乡里暖亦寒。

Nepenthes

The dawn moon breaks through the mist when the stamp of hoofs are swift,
The evening breeze sways dripping willows, and the sound of the flute remains.
Since ancient times, there have been many wars in the border areas,
Therefore,the peaceful hometown makes people feel cold even in warm days.

日 常

沧海桑田时入梦，

青山绿水亦涉足。

万丈红尘三杯茶，

千秋大业一卷书。

Daily Life

As the vicissitudes of the world, I dream,
I have also set foot in the green mountains and clear waters.
Three cups of tea are the containers of the vast world's story,
The great cause of a thousand years lies in a book.

嘲

数九寒天下大雨，

气温虽冷心里喜。

莫论春秋与冬夏，

没有妖霾就阿弥。

Mockery

It rains heavily on the coldest day,

Although the temperature is low, I feel so happy.

Regardless of which season it is,

It will be lucky if there is no smog.

四季谣

春观花雨秋品月，

夏听蛙鸣冬踏雪。

若非雾霾来作妖，

哪个不是好时节。

Four Seasons Ballad

I admire the flower sand rain in spring, the moon in autumn,

I hear the croaking of frogs in summer, and step on the snow in winter.

If it weren't for the smog,

Every season would be a good time.

题粉黛草

非云非雾非花香，
仙子原野秀新装。
他日我若为东君，
与尔共舞度春光。

Poem for Pink Muhly Grass

It is not like clouds, mist, or fragrance of flowers,
It is like a faery shows her new clothes in the field.
If I were the sun—god,
May we would dance together for eternity.

秋　思

金风萧瑟山河秋，

落叶有情应有愁。

故人他乡可安好，

欲问还休思难休。

Autumn Mood

The golden wind rustles through the mountains and rivers in autumn,

Fallen leaves should have their emotions and sorrows.

I wonder if my old friends are all fine in the foreign land,

I hesitate to ask but the missing cannot stop.

秋 夜

月到深秋凉且明，
阴晴圆缺自不同。
北雁南飞鸣空过，
东楼西风添思情。

Autumn Night

In late autumn, the weather is cool and the moon is bright.
Cloudy or sunny, waxing or waning, the moon is different.
Wild geese honk flying to the south,
West wind blows into the east building and brings more missing to people.

咏　秋

金风萧瑟白露降，
月明星稀秋分凉。
伏暑欲问何时返，
应待来年夏至忙。

Ode to Autumn

The autumn wind is soughing and the white dew falls,
The moon is bright, the stars are sparse, and the Autumn Equinox is cool.
Summer heat is asked about its return,
That will be the Summer Solstice next year.

风

闲来无有事，
悄然入我屋。
轻撩杯中茶，
漫翻桌上书。

拥我入柔怀，
亲我肌与肤。
香我心脾肺，
醉我魂灵出。

耳边呢喃语，
枕旁衣帐拂。
醒来曰怅然，
何处去寻汝?

Wind

Having nothing to do,
The wind quietly enters my room,
Gently tease the tea in the cup,
Flip through the books on the table.

Embrace me gently,
Kiss my body.
Bring fragrance to my heart, spleen, and lungs,
Enchant my soul.

Whisper in my ear,
Beside the pillow, the clothes and curtains are brushed.
Waking up and feeling melancholy all day,
Where to find you?

秋

众人皆曰春光好，
我道秋日胜春朝。
谷熟果香禽畜肥，
幸无风雪来打扰。

Autumn

Everyone says that the spring scenery is good,
While I say that autumn is better than spring.
It is a harvest season with ripe grains and fruits,
and fattened poultry and livestock,
Fortunately, there is no wind or snow to disturb.

小暑吟

蝉鸣林下暑意升，
热浪滚滚红尘中。
闭门诗书细品茶，
心间自有清凉风。

Minor Heat Chant

Cicadas chirping in the forest, the summer heat rises,
The scorching heat waves in the world.
When I close the door, read poetry and taste tea,
There is a cool breeze in the heart.

雷雨所至歌

六月雨骤雷轰鸣，
闷我心头事千重。
小屋如笼蚊虫闹，
推窗欲呼万里晴。

Songs of Thunderstorms

In June, the rain falls suddenly and thunder roars,
A thousand confused thoughts come to my mind.
The cabin is like a cage filled with noisy mosquitoes and insects,
Pushing the window, I want to cry for a clear sky.

高　考

孤灯寒窗十二年，
端午时节箭引弦。
一片墨声天未晓，
三更鸡鸣人始眠。
书中瀚海千里外，
卷里乾坤方寸间。
笔下龙蛇腹有稿，
摘星成竹指九天。

College Entrance Examination

After twelve years of diligent study,
During the Dragon Boat Festival, the exam will begin.
The sky is as black as ink at dawn,
The candidates fall asleep in the dead of night when rooster crows.
In the book, the knowledge has no bounds,
In the paper, what they have learned could be tested.
The candidates make mental preparation before they write smoothly,
And they will succeed in passing the examination with high grades.

小满吟

人生最愿是小满，

花蕾初绽月尚圆。

后有高山前有路，

不惧妖魔不慕仙。

Lesser Fullness of Grain Chant

My greatest wish in life is not too full,

The flower buds are blooming and the moon is still round.

With mountains behind my back and roads in front of me,

I'm not afraid of demons and do not admire immortals.

故乡行

杨柳轻扬送冬归，
东风拂煦携春回。
人欢车快返故乡，
一路歌声紧相随。

喜鹊叫呵燕子舞，
流水潺潺桃喷蕊。
新房成排田成方，
催春锣鼓声声脆。

飞车驰过火龙岗，
机器轰鸣镐锹飞。
群众汗水引清泉，
喝令龙王听指挥。

眼前又越老碱坡，
满目碧绿欲滴翠。
“银色世界”不复返，
不毛荒地禾苗肥。

黄沙滩前极目眺，
枣树棵棵笑微微。
牧童响鞭致敬意，
喜迎远客故乡回。

一条金路向太阳，
两旁白杨队连队。
可曾记得羊肠道？
怎知昔日乱坟堆？

乍看一眼将曾相识呵，
细看两下又惭愧。
老区容颜日日新，
天工巧手难描绘！

返故乡呵故乡行，
车轮滚滚激情汇。
迎着春风歌一曲，
声声醉得人心碎。

Hometown Tour

Willows gently bid farewell to winter,
The warm east wind brings spring back.
People enjoy driving back to their hometown,
The singing accompanies us along the way.

The magpies chatter and swallows dance,
Flowing water murmurs, and peach blossoms are full—blown.
The new houses are arranged in rows and the fields are square,
A loud gong and drum roll, which urges spring to come early.

Driving by Huolonggang, I see,
The machine roaring and the shovel flying.
People work hard to draw clear springs,
And order the Dragon King to follow orders.

When I arrive at the Laojian Slope,
Green color is everywhere.
The silver world will never return,
The barren land is fertile for grass seedlings.

I gaze out from afar at the yellow sandy beach,
Jujube trees smile faintly.
The shepherd boy honks his whip in tribute,
Welcoming guests back to their hometown happily from far away.

A golden path goes towards the sun,
The white poplar squadrons stand on both sides.
Do you remember the intestines?
How to know the chaotic graves in the past?

At first glance, we may have met before,
Take a closer look and feel ashamed.
The old district's appearance is getting better and better day by day,
Even craftsman in heaven cannot describe such a scene!

Returning to my hometown and visiting my hometown,
The wheels roll with passion.
Sing a song in the spring breeze,
The sounds overwhelmed me.

题芍药

牡丹花罢芍药开，
不争春色富贵彩。
千姿百态令人怜，
妩媚娇艳芳自来。

Poem for Paeonia lactiflora

Paeonia flowers bloom after peonies,
Do not strive for the wealth and splendor of spring.
The various forms are lovely,
Charming, graceful, and fragrant.

游酉阳桃花源

昔日伟贤赋诗篇，
今朝西东考证难。
陶令已去桃花谢，
空余游人寻耕田。

Tour of Youyang Peach Garden

In the past, great sages wrote poems for it,
Today it's difficult to identify the location.
Yuanming Tao has passed away and peach blossoms have fallen,
Leaving tourists searching for the farmland.

夜 聚

月挂水中天，
水飘天上月。
桥侧聚同窗，
议政逞人杰。

注释：晚游，因按大家所定规格，即席乘兴赋之。

Night Gathering

The moon's reflection is in the water,
The water lies as if in the sky.
Beside the bridge the classmates gather,
Talking about politics actively as if they were great people.

Note: A night tour, it is improvised and written according to the specification set by everyone.

喻　儿

常与同好细磋商，

也向傻瓜指方向。

今朝弹琴牛不知，

他日或可思雅量。

Advice to My Son

Regularly consult with your friends,

Give directions to the fools, as well.

Today, my son can't understand my intentions,

He will consider it one day.

赠学子

窗前竹摇案上书，
三更明月帐中屋。
待到金鸡白天下，
笔走龙蛇脱颖出。

To Students

Read books beside the window, bamboo outside swaying,
Study late at night with moon bright.
A new day has started when the roosters crow,
You will write your papers smoothly.

闲 事

塞翁失马焉非福，
亡羊补牢犹未晚。
心胸开阔挥手去，
明日还是艳阳天。

Idle Matters

A blessing in disguise is also a blessing,
It's never too late to mend.
With an open mind, wave your hand,
Tomorrow is still a sunny day.

暮　春

杨柳春还在，
落花拂面来；
遥知此非雪，
仍慕咏絮才。

Late Spring

It's still spring here because willows remain,
Falling flowers brush against my face,
Remotely, I know that this is not snow,
Still I admire the poet who eulogized the willow catkins.

观杨丽萍《莲花心》

亦妖亦仙亦人怪，
此舞只应梦里来。
公孙胡姬皆羞愧，
哪辨凡间与世外。

Watching Yang Liping's "Lotus Heart"

They are both demons, immortals, and spirits,
This dance should only exist in a dream.
Gongsun and Huji shall be all ashamed,
Who can distinguish between the mortal world
and the outside world.

别少亭

一日相见如故人，

两月共处增情分。

此去别君三千里，

四海之内存知音。

Farewell to My Friend Shaoting

Just for one day we meet each other like old friends,

Two months together our friendship have become even deeper.

Three thousand miles from here after this farewell,

I will miss you wherever you are.

别伊洛

滚滚伊河寄深情，
巍巍仙阁增思忧。
我恋山水不忍去，
几番催促几回头。

Good—bye, Yiluo River

The rolling Yiluo River carries deep affection,
And the towering Faerie Pavilion makes it deeper.
As loving mountains and rivers, I'm reluctant to leave,
Though being urged, I turn back my head for times.

迎春花

正月雨雪卷地湿，
莺啼燕舞未有时。
莫道天地无暖意，
迎春花开第一枝。

Winter Jasmine

In the first month of the lunar year, the ground is very muddy because of the rainy and snowy day,
The singing of birds and the dancing of swallows have disappeared.
Do not say that it has no warmth in the world,
The winter jasmines have bloomed.

古河（二首）

其　一

一湾秽水几多愁，
难煞数任贤良州。
试问当年大禹事，
可曾对汝摊双手？

其　二

今番新官又上任，
誓言水清河去臭。
但愿此次能成真，
还你真身数风流。

Ancient River (Two Poems)

No.1

How much sorrow does a bay of polluted water bring,
It is a great trouble for severed local officials.
I would like to know whether the Great Yu, facing the flood,
While did nothing.

No.2

The new official has taken office this time,
Vowed to clear the river and eliminate its odor.
I hope the pledge can really come true,
Then the official would be remembered by people.

和陆游《临安春雨初霁》

世味年来薄似纱，
也曾骑马客京华。
小楼一夜听秋雨，
最是富士话桑麻。

车行三刻闲作草，
机翔千里细品茶。
锦衣再引风尘叹，
犹及春分到我家。

Answer "The Clear Day after Spring Rain in Lin'an" by Lu You

Friendship is worldly as thin as yarn for years,
I also rode horses to visit Lin'an.
Listening to the autumn rain all night in the little building,
And talked about farm life with others.
After hours of driving, I feel bored and practice handwriting,
After flying thousands of miles, I taste tea.
Do not worry that the wind and dust would make the beautiful clothes dirty again,
Until the Spring Equinox, I will arrive at my hometown.

春

无风无尘亦无霜，

一层花雨一层芳。

十里桃花十里情，

百鸟争鸣百花香。

千山有水千岭秀，

万木病殁万壑苍。

年年昌平岁岁新，

宇域澄清又春光。

Spring

No wind, no dust, no frost,

A layer of flowers brings a layer of fragrance.

Ten miles of peach blossoms means lots of romantic relationship,

A hundred birds chirping and a hundred flowers fragrant.

A thousand mountains have water, and a thousand ridges are beautiful,

Ten thousand trees perish, and ten thousand ravines are desolate.

Every year is prosperous and new,

Everywhere is clear and full of sunlight in spring.

归故乡

归心似箭穿云天，

双脚生风犹嫌慢。

故乡故人故情谊，

驱我快马再加鞭。

Return to Hometown

The eagerness to get back home is like an arrow piercing through the clouds,

I still feel slow even if I drive so fast.

Hometown, old friends and ties of friendship

Drive me faster and faster.

咏　茶

日月精华叶底藏，

静心洗浴露容妆。

窗外闲风随冷暖，

壶中清友自芬芳。

Ode to Tea

The essence of the sun and the moon is stored at the bottom of the tea leaves.

Take a bath and wait peacefully, it will show its ture shape.

There is no need to mind whether the breeze outside the window is cold or warm,

Just enjoy the fragrance from the pot of tea.

雾 凇

非雪非霜也非冰，
银装素裹仰雾凇。
莫叹世事皆浊物，
去腐化朽有精灵。

Rime

Not snow, not frost, not even ice,
The tall rime is like being covered with silver.
Do not sigh that all things in the world are sordid,
The rime has the magic to make it clean.

赠　友

岁月如歌亦峥嵘，
实时奋进何须停。
莫道人生路漫漫，
应知有雨也有风。
留得心中阳光媚，
沿途无处不风景。
挥手潇洒有时光，
你我且行且从容。

于2024年7月3日

To a Friend

Time flows like a song, and it is also an extraordinary period,
We must advance bravely and, never pause.
Do not lament life's road so long and winding,
For rain and wind will come during the long journey.

Keep sunshine bright within your heart,
Then sceneries are along the road.
Wave goodbye to my friend, we will meet someday,
You and I keep going leisurely.

July 3, 2024

夏　至

蝉鸣声声迎夏至，
荷风阵阵送暑来。
麦收锣鼓已收场，
只待秋实唱开怀。

于 2024 年 6 月 28 日

Summer Solstice

The continuous chirping of cicadas welcomes the Summer Solstice,
The intermittent breeze blows though lotus brings the heat back.
The wheat harvest drums have ceased,
I am just waiting for the autumn fruits to sing and celebrate.

June 28, 2024

辑二

Section Ⅱ

现代诗

Modern Poetry

Section Ⅱ

路

我们没有崩溃倒塌，

我们也不是威胁的童话。

不怕地球村里的唱衰和抹黑，

岁月悠悠我们都在这里，

不管捧杀还是棒杀。

行大道，

民为本，

民之所望就是政之精华。

利天下，

民为邦，

本固邦宁方为人间桑麻。

这是我的国，

这是我的家。

走自己选择的路，

不过多在意别人，

无聊的指点还是闲话。

于 2024 年 6 月 20 日

The Path

We have not crumbled, nor have we fallen,
We are not the fairy tale of threat theory.
Without the fear of denying and bad—mouthing from the global village,
We are still what we are when time flies,
No matter the assessment is criticism or extolment.

Walk on the right path,
and put the people's well—being first,
Because the hopes of them are the essence of governance.
Benefit the people.
and people will be the root of the nation,
Because the stability of them brings peace and happy life.

This is my country,
This is my hometown.
Walk the path we've chosen,
Unbothered by others,
No matter pointless opinions or boring chatters.

June 20, 2024

蝉

在地下待了三年，
从不抱怨时光的黑暗。
奋力向地平线靠近，
终于换来夏日生命的展现。

风雨是生命的洗礼，
酷暑是成长的彼岸。
不枉阅了一次人世，
尽管知道岁月的短暂。

挥臂欢快地生活，
开口尽情地歌唱盛宴，
给季节增添光彩，
把音韵留给人间。

于 2024 年 7 月 15 日

Cicada

For three years underground you stay,
Never complain about the darkness.
Striving toward the horizon's line,
You earn a summer's brief, bright life.

The wind and rain, life's baptism,
The scorching heat, growth's distant shore.
It is worth to glimpsing the world,
Although it is known as a short time.

Waving wings when you dance,
Singing the songs as you wish.
You add your light to summer's glow,
And leave your song for all around.

July 15, 2024

致某些人

你和他讲道义，
他给你讲利益；
你和他讲利益，
他给你讲国家；
你给他讲国家，
他给你讲法律；
你和他讲法律，
他给你讲权力；
你和他讲权力，
他给你讲自由；
你和他讲自由，
他给你讲道义。
噫吁嚱，
是非标准就是我说了算 ，
契约就是你没有权益。

于 2024.7.10.

To Certain People

You talk to him about morality,
He talks about interests in return;
You talk to him about interests,
He talks about the nation in retain;
You talk to him about the nation,
He talks about the law in retain;
You talk to him about the law,
He talks about power in retain;
You talk to him about power,
He talks about freedom in retain;
You talk to him about freedom,
He talks about morality in retain.
Alas!
The standard of right or wrong is formulated by me,
And the contract means you have no rights.

July 10, 2024

霜 降

碧云天，

水波寒翠烟。

叶落叠成诗，

雁南飞，无鸣蝉。

橘黄枫红菊飘香，

霜降人间。

露深蟹肥稻菽归仓，

竹枝从容暖向寒，

风骨依然。

于 2024.10.25.

First Frost

In the autumn, sky is bright blue,

The water appears green and turns cold with verdant mist.

As autumn leaves fall, they form a poem in layers.
Geese fly southward, and the chirping of summer's cicadas has disappeared.
The orange citrus, red maple, and fragrance of chrysanthemums exude autumn's essence.
As frost descends upon the world,
The deep autumn dews highlight the plump crabs and harvested grains.
Bamboo branches gracefully accept the change from the warm towards the cold,
Their essence unchanged.

On October 25th, 2024.

豆腐吟

你可以不爱我，
却离不开我。
虽难登大雅厅堂，
依然温馨着你的饭桌。

没有花容月貌，
无损如玉清白、素颜品格。
不凝思，豆浆一杯，
切成片，煎炒琥珀。

不要嫌我苦涩，
不要骂我软弱，
即使把我捣碎、生吃，
仍是美味一个。

哪怕你将我封藏，
发霉了，仍然有人爱我。
我有我的能量，
你无法抛弃我。

Tofu Chant

You cannot love me,
But you cannot do without me.
Although it is not suited for high—end restaurants,
It is always a common dish, which warms the ordinary people's daily life.

It does not have a beautiful appearance,
Which brings no damage to its character and morals of plain jade.
Before being made into a shape it is a cup of soybean milk,
Being cut into slices, it could be stired and fried.

Do not dislike me because of bitterness,
Do not scold me for being soft and weak,
Even if you crush me and eat me raw,
Still I'm delicious.

Even if you seal me up,
Even though I'm moldy, there are still people who love me.
I have my energy,
You cannot abandon me.

岁月的歌

岁月是公平的种子，
埋在哪里就在哪里开花结果。
勤勤恳恳它会给你奖励，
浑浑噩噩它会让你蹉跎。

追求所爱、遗忘所失
注重当下，珍惜所得。
你对它有多少珍爱，
你就有多少收获。

过往不恋，未来不惧
当下不负，方能踏平坎坷。
只要你不躺平，
时光的艰难困苦能奈你何。

前进的每一滴汗水，
会留有或深或浅的脚窝。
认真生活，哪怕速度慢些，
岁月也会展现应有的彩色。

Song of Time

Time is the seed of fairness,
Wherever it is buried, it will bloom and bear fruit.
Living seriously will reward you,
Or you will waste your time on the opposite.

Pursue what one loves and forget what one has lost.
Pay attention to the present and cherish what you have gained.
How much you cherish it,
you will get what you want.

No longing in the past, no fear in the future.
Only living up to the present can we overcome obstacles.
As long as you do not lie down,
Any difficulty and hardship will not defeat you.

Every effort forward
Will leave some deep or shallow footprints.
Live diligently and sincerely, even if the speed is a little bit slow,
Time will show its color.

打工者

眼神中，有时闪烁无助和迷茫，
蕴藏不甘和坚韧。
面对失业压力、生活困顿，
依旧保持对未来渴望。
脚下城市或许不是归宿，
手中工作仍然是家人的脊梁。

追寻自己的未来，
不放弃每一次的起航。
虽有遗憾。没有惆怅。
心之所向便是暖阳。
他们也许不是最耀眼的星光，
却是岁月的脚步、社会的肩膀。

相信痛苦和汗水必将有助，
生活不会刻意赖账。
眼下的阴影，
或在不远处洒下阳光。
愿所有的理想如期而至，
愿他们的努力将现实照亮。

Workers

Their eyes
Sometimes flicker helplessness and confusion,
They also contain the power of unwillingness and resilience.
Faced the pressure of unemployment and the difficulties of life,
They still keep faith for the future.
The city beneath their feet may not be their destination,
While the work they do is still the backbone of their families.

In order to pursue their own future,
They wait for the next departure, never give up.
although regrets remain, while without melancholy.
The direction of the heart is warm sunshine.
They may not be the most dazzling starlight.
But they are the time's footsteps and society's shoulders.

Pain and sweat will definitely help,
Life will never deliberately cheat hardworking people.
The shadow right now
May scatter sunlight at the place not far away.
May all ideals come as scheduled,
May their efforts illuminate the reality.

谁病了

那天你认真地对我说，
你病了，认知错乱。
我惊愕地呆住，
不知道是该笑还是该烦。

虽不严重，你病了多年，
包容你，顺其自然。
我笑你太疯癫，
你说我看不穿。

固执有固执的权利，
善良有善良的凄惨。
无知有无知的快乐，
明智有明智的黑暗。

究竟是我还是你病了，
大家多次劝你去医院。
你病了却让我吃药，
苦笑，北辙南辕。

Who Is Sick

You told me seriously that day,
You were sick and had a cognitive disorder.
I was shocked,
Do not know whether I should laugh or worry.

Although it's not serious, you've been sick for many years,
I tolerate you and let things slide.
I laugh at you for being too mad,
You say I can't see through and understand.

Stubbornness has the right of stubbornness,
Kindness has its own tragedy.
Ignorance brings joy,
Wisdom has its darkness.

Who is ill on earth, you or me?
Relatives and friends have repeatedly advised you to go to hospital.
Instead of asking me to take medicine when you are sick,
Pole apart, I have nothing to do but smile bitterly.

你　好

你的笑容温暖过我的眼神，
我曾闪耀在你心中的夜晚。
不必问候、不必祝福，
知心无需语言，
知己常在心间。

举头仰望苍穹，
遥寄深情思念。
不妨心怀一抔阳光，
与星辰把盏，
与岁月言欢。

Hello

Your smile warmed my eyes,
I once shone in your heart at some night.
No need to greet or bless,
Understanding requires no language,
A confidant is always in the heart.

Looking up at the sky,
I send deep affection afar.
May I have a handful of sunshine in my heart,
Raising a cup to the stars,
Cheering with time.

致女性

你是高山的峡谷，
虽然不易显露风光，
没有你，
就不会有小溪和道路。

你是皇天的后土，
孕育了世上的花草禾木，
没有你，
就没有人类和生物。

你是流动的柔水，
善良包容滋润甜美着万物，
没有你，
生命难以延续、星球干枯。

你是美丽和慈悲的化身，
给人间带来希望和光簇，
没有你，
世上的一切美好惨不忍睹。

你是天的另一半，

撑起家国世界的梁柱，

致敬女性！

致敬，人类之母！

To Women

You are the canyon of a high mountain,

Although it is not easy to showcase the scenery,

Without you,

There will be no streams or roads.

You nourish the soil,

Nurturing the flowers, grass and trees of the world,

Without you,

There will be no humans or animals.

You are the flowing water,

Your kindness, tolerance, and sweetness nourish all things,

Without you,

Life is difficult to sustain and the planet dries up.

You are the incarnation of beauty and compassion,
Bringing hope and light to the world,
Without you,
All the beauty in the world is unwatchable.

You are the other half of the sky,
Supporting the family and the world,
Salute Women!
Salute, Mother of Human Beings!

卖粽者

朔风是一只近旁的狮子，
飞雪如一个巨大的帐篷。
鸦雀躲在树枝上瑟瑟发抖，
人们裹紧棉衣，炉火通红。

“卖粽子的来了，谁要粽子？”
一声响亮的叫卖，
增添了一丝烟火气息，
打破了街上的沉闷幽静。

为生意不在意每一个冷漠，
为生活不辜负每一次热情。
邻居们谈笑：
他成了咱这一片儿的网红。

Zongzi Seller

North wind is like a lion nearby,
The flying snow is like a huge tent.
Crows and sparrows are hiding in the tree, trembling and shivering,
People wrap themselves tightly in cotton clothes, and the fire turns red.

"Here comes the Zongzi seller. Who wants Zongzi?"
A loud cry of selling
Adds a little bit flaver of life,
Breaks the dullness and silence on the street.

For business he does not care about any indifference,
Kindness and inclusiveness nourish and sweeten everything.
Neighbors chat and laugh:
He has become an internet celebrity in our neighborhood.

秋天的故事

一眨眼夏天成了黄叶，
一转身秋天成了今天。
又是一年金风雄起，
又闻星夜蟋蟀幽怨。

经过了春天的滋润，
经历了酷暑的熬煎。
收获了天地的成果，
记下了岁月的礼赞。

太理性难越柴米油盐河，
太感性难过风花雪月关。
秋天面临着严冬的考验，
如何迎来涅槃的春天？

心静方能听见自己的心声，
心平才能看清万物的本源。
心中有爱才能穿透风云，
心底无私才能眼有河山。

非饱经风霜不能百炼成钢，
非咬紧牙关岂能一往无前。
用宽广的心胸接纳现在，
用探索的心态迎接明天。

遍野的稻菽就是动力，
过去的风雨不必悲观。
只有走好当下的每一步，
才能给未来留下最美的纪念。

季节里的风霜雨雪，
渲染了脚下的沧海桑田。
心若不动风又奈何。
你若不伤岁月无憾。

有风景不任性大道至简，
怀大义利天下顺应大自然。
把握好自己的节奏和轨道，
一定会穿越前方的冬天。

叶绿叶黄莫空悲叹，

匆匆流年渐逝云烟。

愿历经春秋无愧信念，

愿时光静好世间安然。

Story of Autumn

In the blink of an eye, summer has turned into
Yellow leaves,
Turning around, autumn has come.
It's time for another's golden wind blowing.
I have heard again the crickets chirping with worrying and complaining at night.

After the nourishment of spring,
Having experienced the intense heat.
Having reaped the fruits of the heaven and the earth,
I record the praise of time.

Being too rational makes it difficult to face reality,
Being too emotional makes it hard to pass the test of romantic relationship.
Autumn faces the ordeals of severe winter,

How to welcome the new spring?

Only by keeping calm can one hear one's own voice in heart,
Peace of mind is the key to seeing the origin of all things.
Only with love in heart can one penetrate the storms,
Only with selflessness in the heart can one have rivers and mountains in his eyes.

Without being weathered by wind and frost, one cannot be strong and brave,
Without gritting one's teeth, one cannot move forward with progress.
Embrace the present with a broad heart,
Greet tomorrow with an exploratory mindset.

The rice beans everywhere are the driving force,
There is no need to be pessimistic about the storms in the past.
Only by taking every step of the present well,
Can we leave the most beautiful memories for the future.

The wind, frost, rain, and snow in the season,
Sentimentalize the ever—changing world beneath my feet.
If the heart does not move, what can the wind do.
If you're not sad, time has no regrets.

There is scenery in heart, and great truths are often simple

Embrace righteousness and benefit the world
by adapting to nature.
Grasp our own rhythm and track,
We will definitely get through the winter.

Green leaves, yellow leaves, do not sigh,
The fleeting years gradually fade away.
May we even be filled with unwavering faith
after experiencing a lot of things,
May we have good years and peaceful life.

老门岗

风雨中有他的身影，
严寒里有他的咳声。
清晨有他孤独的忍耐，
深夜有他巡回的走动。

虽然手脚已不再矫健，
人们梦里他安稳如钟。
曾独自力阻违规之举，
为值班常吃残茶冷羹。

不缺吃穿，儿女求他安享晚年，
他有自己的打算—
“咱农村人闲不住，
多少总得做点事情。”

人生的歌有高有低也有新声，
生活的茶有苦有香也有平静。
岁月本来不易，
他不渴求别人的理解和认同。

年复一年日复日，

送走了夏，迎来了冬。

秋霜染白了他的鬓角，

春风绽开了皱纹的笑容。

Old Doorman

His figure is seen in the wind and rain,
His cough is heard in the severely cold days.
The morning sees his solitary patience,
The late night listens to his walking around.

Although his hands and feet are no longer agile,
People dream while he remains at his post.
He once tried his best to resist any irregularities by himself,
He often drinks leftover tea and eats cold soup for duty.

No shortage of food and clothing, his children want him to enjoy his old age peacefully,
But he has his own plans
"We rural people are not idle,
Should always find something to do. "

Life has its ups and downs, even new changes as well,
Life is like the tea which contains bitterness, fragrance, and calmness.
Time has never been easy,
He does not expect for understanding and recognition from others.

Year after year, day after day,
He bids farewell to summer and welcomes winter.
The autumn frost has whitened his temples,
However,the spring breeze smoothes his wrinkles.

盲 师

虽然没有眼睛，
依然在黑暗中寻找光明。
不认命选择了按摩，
不服输认定了刻苦用功。

好手艺是钥匙和光束，
打开生意与家庭的美景。
汗水与坚持的力量，
让常人眼中充满尊敬。

坚守良知的岁月，
一次治愈决不让二次返程。
不挣有失良心的钱财，
正是一些有眼睛者缺失的真诚。

虽然看不到世界，
心中却充满彩色和光明。
守住手艺、善良而利他人，
谱写出国家级荣誉的美称。

只有握紧真、善，

事业才有灿烂前程；

只要胸中洒满阳光，

生活会有无限风景。

Blind Massagist

Although blind,
I am still searching for light in the dark.
Not accepting the fate, I choose to be a massagist.
Not accepting being defeated, I firmly believe in working hard.

Good craftsmanship is the key and a beam of light,
which opens the nice view of business and family.
The power of sweat and perseverance,
Get full respect from other people's eyes.

In the years of upholding conscience,
One healing never needs a second return.
Not earning dishonest money
Is the sincerity that some people with eyes lack of.

Although I cannot see the world,

My heart is filled with colors and light.
Maintain the craftsmanship, be kind and benefit others,
Compose a life song of national honors.

Only the heart is filled with sincerity,
Could the career have a bright future;
As long as my chest is filled with sunshine,
Life must have infinite scenery.

我是一只猫头鹰

熬了多少黄昏，
起了多少五更，
不管风雨霜雪，
不论春夏秋冬；
为了收获一个金色的未来，
除尽九州的鼠患邪佞，
呵，我是一只猫头鹰。

明月知道我有王安石的才华，
晨星知道我有比干的忠诚，
春花知道我有文天祥的热血，
秋实知道我有包公的刚正，
鼠雀知道我有达摩克利斯之剑，
晚霞知道我有普罗米修斯之勇；
哦，我有大海一样的胸怀，
呵，我有白云一样的豪情。

也许昼眠被看成了孤傲，
也许搏击的翅膀惹了闲风，

也许歌唱的喉舌凄厉刺耳，
也许猛进的方式不苟世情；
世俗们说我是丧门灾星，
亲朋们说我是千年冤种，
顽愚的冷弹时时射入我的身躯，
阴毒的大网处处窥伺我的身影……

即使一时不能被人理解，
是鹰就要有鹰的心灵，
是鹰就要有鹰的追求，
是鹰就要有鹰的啸鸣。
哪怕它阴云密布风狂雨猛，
难改我意志如铁一片初衷。
看东方，知识的阳光已将愚昧驱散，
“爱鸟”的春风已奉还我应有的羽翎。

呵，我是一只猫头鹰，
一只腐朽畏惧的精灵！

I Am an Owl

so many sleepless dusks,
so many mornings of early getting up,
Regardless of wind, rain, frost, or snow,
Regardless of spring, summer, autumn, and winter;
In order to harvest a bright future,
Eliminate all rat infestations and evil tongues,
Oh, I am an owl.

The bright moon knows that I am a talent as Wang Anshi,
Morning Star knows that I am as loyal as Bigan,
Spring flowers know that I am as passionate as Wen Tianxiang,
Autumn fruits know that I am as right—minded as Bao Zheng,
Sparrows and mice know that I have the sword of Damocles,
The sunset glow knows that I have the courage like Prometheus;
Oh, I have a heart like the sea,
Oh, I have the enthusiastic as white clouds.

Perhaps daydreaming is seen as aloof,
Perhaps the wings of the fight have stirred up the idle wind,

Perhaps the singing voice is sad and piercing,
Perhaps the aggressive approach is inhuman;
The common people say I am a jinx,
Relatives and friends say that I am a great,
Stupid and stubborn cold bullets constantly hit my body,
The insidious web is everywhere peeping at my figure...

Even if it cannot be understood at the moment,
If you were an eagle, you should have an eagle's heart,
If you were an eagle, you should have the eagle's pursuit,
If you were an eagle, you would have the eagle's roar.
Even if it is shrouded in dark clouds, with strong winds and rain,
It's hard to change my will, as if it were an iron original intention.
Look to the East, the sunshine of knowledge has already dispelled ignorance,
The spring breeze of loving birds has returned my rightful feathers.

Oh, I'm an owl,
An elf of the decay years!

夜 市

一盏灯、两盏灯……
天上落下一群星。
一群星、两群星……
一条银河流进城。

这里——烟糖百货小五金，
那里——土产服装小餐厅……
人的海呵货的山，
笑的潮呵春的风。

星光里鲤鱼跳龙门，
金辉下彩蝶舞群红。
一货一物一颗心，
一餐一茶一片情。

不怕雾，不怕风，
乌云越压灯越明。
牛郎织女惊相叹：
“天上星，不如地上灯！”

啊，一盏灯、两盏灯……

银河涌进座座城。

夜市灯火映万家，

迎来朝霞东方红。

Night Market

One lamp, two lamps...
They are the group of stars falling from the sky.
A group of stars, two groups of stars
A Milky Way flows into the city.

Here—tobacco, sugar and hardware,
There—local specialty,clothing, small restaurants...
So many people and so many goods,
The tide of laughter and the wind of spring.

In the starlight, carp jump over the dragon gate,
Under the golden glow, colorful butterflies dance in groups.
One product, one object, one heart,
One meal, one cup of tea, one love.

Not afraid of fog, not afraid of wind,
The darker the clouds, the brighter the lights.
The Cowherd and Weaver Girl exclaim in surprise:
"The lights on the ground are brighter than the stars in the sky!"

Ah, one lamp, two lamps...
The Milky Way flows into cities.
The lights in night market illuminate thousands of households,
Welcoming the morning glow and the eastern red.

伏 天

天空一片灰暗，
推开门，
灼浪在身上弥漫。
伸出手，
抹了一把擦不干的汗，
吸口气，
胸口压着一块方砖。

揽一缕湿热的空气，
拧了拧，
雨水哗哗流进禾田。
热让泥土更具能量，
湿让百禾枝茂叶繁，
我仿佛触摸到丰收的秋天。

Dog Days

The sky is a gloomy,
Push open the door,
Heat waves permeate the body.
Extend the hand,
Wipe a handful of sweat that couldn't be wiped dry,
Take a breath,
A square brick is pressed on the chest.

Grab a wisp of damp and hot air,
Twist it,
Rainwater splashes into the fields.
Heat gives the soil more energy,
Moisture makes branches and leaves lusher,
I feel as if I have touched the harvest of autumn.

那颗星

一颗明亮的辰星——雷锋，
一个光辉的身影——雷锋。
每当看到这个名字——雷锋，
就会肃然起敬，心潮难平。

此刻，我仿佛——
看到他在列车上扫地的笑容，
看到他雨夜盖水泥的英姿，
看到他搀扶老大娘的身影，
看到他戴着红领巾在孩子们当中，
看到他月夜练武，独自刻苦用功……
对群众他像春天般的温暖，
对坏人他像严冬一样无情。
春风拂煦，
把雷锋的精神播扬万里;
江河奔腾，
把雷锋的事迹畅怀歌颂。

当我们凝望着蓝天雄鹰，
思考怎样才能不虚度一生，
请打开《雷锋日记》吧，
雷锋会教给我们怎样工作和前行——
“把有限的生命投入到
无限的为人民服务之中”，
为国家可以“牺牲自己的一切，
直至生命”。
雷锋的崇高精神充实着——
我们的理想和前进的豪情。
让我们懂得对人民、对祖国，
要无私无悔、赤胆忠诚；
使我们明白，为名誉地位金钱活着，
是庸俗的哲学、腐朽的人生。

雷锋精神怎样凝成？
用心，用汗，用行动。
驾驶室里，他在一字一句学习，
营房灯下，他在为战友飞针补缝，
风雨途中，他送母子找到亲人，
受灾地区，他寄来无限深情……

钢笔懂得雷锋的“钉子精神”，
油灯知道雷锋的火热心情。
决不做说话的巨人行动的矮子，
是雷锋的写照和心声。
思想和行动是不可分离的兄弟，
他用这个天平将自己量衡。
处处自觉奉献社会、服务大众，
《雷锋日记》的篇章是最好的说明。

一个人做几件好事容易，
难的是不做坏事、做好事终生。
雷锋就是这样一个普通的人，
一个言行一致的伟大标兵。
这样的人古今有几许?
这样的品行中外有几名?
雷锋呵雷锋，
思想境界似漫山遍野的杜鹃花，
道德品质如洁白无瑕的玉晶。
雷锋啊雷锋，
中华儿女道德品格的高峰。

人人都说海阔山高，
依我看，
海阔阔不过雷锋的心胸，
山高高不过雷锋的热情。
工地上带病推砖的脚印，
告诉我们，雷锋的心和祖国相通；
烈火里奋勇扑打的身躯，
告诉我们，雷锋的奉献可逐云摘星。
他以苦为乐、以苦为荣，
头脑里没有个人的私欲，
只有国家、集体、群众。
他用壮丽的青春写下，
热血与理想的交融。
雷锋呵雷锋，
普普通通的一名士兵，
一颗永不生锈的螺丝钉。

雷锋是那样的平凡，
好像就在你、我、他之中；
雷锋是那样的伟大，
好像喜马拉雅的山峰。

一切从脚下的小事做起，
点点滴滴的油彩，
可以描绘出灿烂的风景。
一条真理就在这里出现——
平凡造就非凡的英雄，
伟大包含在细小之中。
雷锋呵雷锋，
时代的光辉榜样，
伟大的普通一兵。

也许有人觉得毫不利己有些傻，
那是不懂大智若愚、大道无形；
也许有人怀疑雷锋精神是否过时，
那是没有理解人类真善美的心灵。
每个人都有自己的世界，
每个人都有自己的路程，
每个人都有自己的价值，
就是实现自我价值的人生。
实现了自身价值的人，
都会成就属于自己的巅峰。
常言道：行为知之成。

一个普通的士兵，
把最普通的事情做成不普通；
一个平凡的人，
把平凡小事做得非凡就是英雄。
雷锋是人间善良与热情的化身，
雷锋是华夏文明的缩影。

啊，描绘雷锋爱憎分明的立场，
可用泰山、北斗；
叙述雷锋言行一致的精神，
可用日月辰星；
颂扬雷锋助人为乐的风格，
可用满山的红花；
歌唱雷锋无私奉献的人生，
可用万里春风！
让我们歌颂吧——
榜样的力量无穷。

君子循道而行，
常患德之不崇。
我们学习雷锋的精神，

需内化于心外化于行。
对崇高理想信念与道德品质的追求，
就是对真善美的传播与践行。
学习雷锋是道德与心灵的交融，
是生命厚度与思想素质的提升；
学雷锋是对民族优良传统的发扬，
是对人类精神财富的传承。
雷锋精神促进社会的和谐、和睦与和平，
雷锋精神促进一种温暖的油然而生。
雷锋精神永存，
雷锋将永生！

看今朝，
青松更青梅更红，
神州大地气象新，
雷锋精神呵，千人学，万人颂。
君不见助人为乐蔚然成风，
君不见跨越了国界和时空。
此刻，我看到——
千千万万志愿者在自发地行动：
雷锋在聚精会神地操纵着数字机床，

雷锋在边防哨卡眼神警惕，
雷锋在麦田驾驶着收割机，
雷锋在科研室研发着编程……
我看到无数个雷锋茁壮成长，
似雨后新笋，江潮涌。

我们的祖国在前进，
脚步铿锵呵万马奔腾。
朋友啊您请看，
在实现中华文明传承的大道上，
那颗永远闪烁的明星，
正是伟大的普通战士，
我们的光辉榜样——
雷锋！

That Star

A bright morning star—Lei Feng,
A shining figure—Lei Feng.
Whenever I see this name—Lei Feng,

I will be filled with reverence, and excited to calm down.

At this moment, I feel as if——
Seeing his smile when he swept the floor on the train,
Seeing his heroic demeanor of covering concrete in rainy nights,
Seeing him supporting the old lady with his hands,
Seeing him wearing a red scarf among the children,
Seeing him practicing Kung fu on a moonlit night, working hard alone...
His warmth to the masses is like spring,
He is ruthless towards bad people like a harsh winter.
The spring breeze is gentle,
Spreading Lei Feng's spirit for thousands of miles;
Rivers surge,
Celebrating the stories of Lei Feng with great enthusiasm.

As we gaze at the eagle in the blue sky,
Thinking about how not to waste the life,
Please open "Lei Feng's Diary",
Lei Feng will teach us how to work and move forward——
"Devote" limited life to
the infinite service for the people,
To sacrifice everything for the country,
Even life.
Lei Feng's noble spirit enriches——
Our ideals and the courage to move forward.
Let us understand how to treat the people and the

motherland,
Let us be selfless, unrepentant, and loyal with courage;
Let us understand that living for fame, status, and money,
is a vulgar philosophy and a decadent life.

How was the spirit of Lei Feng condensed?
With heart, sweat, and action.
In the cab, he was learning word by word,
Under the barracks light, he was sewing for his comrades with flying needles,
On the journey of wind and rain, he helped a mother and son to find each other,
To the disaster—stricken area, he sent his affectionateness,
Pen understands Lei Feng's "nail spirit",
The oil lamp knows Lei Feng's passionate mood.
Actions speak louder than words,
Which is the reflection of Lei Feng.
Thought and action are inseparable brothers,
He often uses this scale to weigh himself.
Consciously dedicating himself to society and serving the public everywhere,
The words in "Lei Feng's Diary" are the best explanation.

It's easy for one person to do a few good things,
The difficulty is not doing bad things and doing good things for the whole life.
Lei Feng is such an ordinary person,
A great model with consistent words and actions.

How many people are there like this in ancient and nowadays?
How many are there at home and abroad for such conduct?
Lei Feng, Lei Feng,
His ideological level is like the azaleas scattered throughout the mountains and fields,
Moral qualities are like pure and flawless jade crystals.
Lei Feng, Lei Feng,
The peak of moral character among Chinese people.

Everyone says that the sea is vast and the mountains are high,
In my opinion,
The vast sea is not as broad as Lei Feng's heart,
The mountains are not as high as Lei Feng's enthusiasm.
He still laid bricks on the construction site while sick,
Which tells us that Lei Feng's heart is connected to his motherland;
The body fighting bravely in the flames,
Which tells us that Lei Feng's dedication could drive the clouds and pick stars.
He took pleasure in suffering and took pride in it,
There is no personal desire in his mind,
There is only the state, the collectivity, and the masses.
He wrote with magnificent youth
With the combination of passion and ideals.
Lei Feng, Lei Feng,

An ordinary soldier,
A screw that never rusted.

Lei Feng was so ordinary,
He seems to be among you and me;
Lei Feng was so great,
He seems like a mountain peak in the Himalayas.
Start with small things at your feet,
Drops of oil paint
Can depict brilliant scenery.
A truth appears ——
Ordinary makes extraordinary heroes,
Greatness is contained within small things.
Lei Feng, Lei Feng,
The shining example of the times,
A great ordinary soldier.

Perhaps some people feel that being selfless is a bit foolish,
That is not understanding how great wisdom seems foolish, and the great way is intangible;
Perhaps some people doubt whether Lei Feng's spirit is outdated,
That is not understanding human heart of truth,kindness and beauty.
Everyone has their own world,
Everyone has their own journey.
Everyone has their own value,

It is the life of realizing self—worth.
People who have realized their own value,
Will always achieve their own peaks.
As the saying goes: achievement is known by their behavior,
An ordinary soldier,
Made the most ordinary things extraordinary;
An ordinary person
Who made ordinary small things extraordinary is a hero.
Lei Feng is the embodiment of human kindness and enthusiasm,
Lei Feng is a microcosm of Chinese civilization.

Ah, to discribe Lei Feng's clear stance of love and hate,
Let's use Mount Taishan and the Plough:
To narrate the spirit of Lei Feng's consistent words and actions,
Let's use the sun, the moon and the stars;
To praise Lei Feng's helpful virtues,
Let's use the red flowers all over the mountain;
To eulogize Lei Feng's life of selfless dedication,
Let's use the ten thousand Li of spring breezes.
Let's sing praises——
The power of models is infinite.

A gentleman follows the morality,
Often afraid of a lack of respect for virtue.
To learn from the spirit of Lei Feng,

We need to internalize in the heart and externalize in action.
The pursuit of lofty ideals, beliefs, and moral qualities,
Is the dissemination and practice of truth, goodness, and beauty.
Learning from Lei Feng is a fusion of morality and soul,
Which is also an improvement in the thickness of life and ideological quality.
Learning from Lei Feng is the promotion of the fine traditions of the nation,
Learning from Lei Feng is also an inheritance of human spiritual wealth.
The spirit of Lei Feng promotes the harmony, and peace of society,
The spirit of Lei Feng also promotes the warm feeling of society.
The spirit of Lei Feng endures forever,
Lei Feng will live forever!

Looking at today,
The green pine is greener and the plum is redder,
The whole land presents a new look,
The spirit of Lei Feng is learned and praised by tens of thousands of people.
Have you seen the trend of helping others become popular?
It has crossed national borders and time and space.
At this moment, I see——

Millions of volunteers are spontaneously taking actions:
They are operating the digital machine tools with great concentration,
They are keeping watchful eyes on the border posts.
They are driving a harvester in the wheat field,
They are developing programming in the research room...
I have seen countless people like Lei Feng growing,
Like new bamboo shoots after rain, and the spring river surges.

Our motherland is developing,
The footsteps are resounding, and ten thousand horses are galloping.
Friend, please take a look,
On the road of achieving the inheritance of Chinese civilization,
The star that twinkles forever,
It is the great ordinary warrior,
Our shining example——
Lei Feng!

诗的婚姻

岁月里，诗歌与国际接轨，
嫁给富豪也别忘了自己是谁。
希望有个好的后代，
别让邯郸学步再次蒙灰。

切莫吮吸了别人的奶渣，
丢掉了自己年华的优美。
切莫满足了自我的心灵欲望，
抛弃了现实生活语言的花蕾。

不要埋怨商业大潮的退去，
不要叹息民众不满的口水。
如果忘了自己的来处，
必然失去应有的地位。

请记住：师夷承古创新当下，
才能刻画出华夏文明的丰碑。
越是民族独有的枝条，
越绽出世界园林可贵的花卉。

Marriage of Poetry

During the years, poetry is in line with international standards,
When marrying a wealthy person, do not forget who you are.
I hope you have good descendants,
They will not follow suit simply.

Do not accept all uncritically,
And forget your own beauty.
Never satisfy your own spiritual desires,
And abandon the flower buds of real life language.

Do not complain about the ebb of business trends,
Do not sigh at the public's dissatisfaction.
If you forget your place of coming,
You will inevitably lose your rightful position.

Please remember: learning from the ancient and overseas, also innovating at present
Is the only way to depict the monument of Chinese civilization.
The more unique the branches are to the nation,
The more precious the flowers are in the world's gardens.

致远方（组诗）

生　活

一个人的生命和生活，
构成了一个人的人生。
生活是生命与活动的组合，
它不但需要健康的身体，
更需要劳动、运动和行动。
世上没有轻而易举的幸福生活，
也没有简单易行的成功人生。
要想获得说走就走的潇洒，
需放弃许多的安逸和宁静；
想获得风和日丽、鲜花掌声，
需不惧风雨如磐、踔厉前行。
你若善待生活它也会给你馈赠，
馈赠就隐藏在你每天的努力之中。
所有看似幸运的事情，
其实都是厚积薄发的结晶。

有人说生活就像开水，

不论冷热，只要合适的温度就行；
有人说生活就像口味，
不论酸甜苦辣，只要合适的口感就行；
有人说生活就像季节，
不论春夏秋冬，只要合适的心情就行。
其实不管甘于寂寞还是不甘寂寞，
只要遵从公理适合自己就行。
生活不需要比别人更好，
但要每天都比过去的自己优胜。

生活中每个人都会有梦想，
梦想让你采取更多的行动。
也许现实支撑不了梦想，
但梦想却可以支撑余生。
梦想虽然是个柔软的词语，
只要你相信就能抵抗现实的坚硬。
许多时候决定生活状态的是信念，
生活里只要梦想还在，
就会让努力的另一个名字叫做成功。

生活的道路总是崎岖不平，

只要多一份理解和从容，
在灰暗的日子里，
也可以看到特殊的风景。
能战胜困苦的是乐观和热爱，
人生因有目标充满动力。
心中有爱有梦想，
日子就会风生水起。
没有迎接不来的春天，
没有到达不了的远方，
只要你朝着理想勇往直行。

生活不会一直风平浪静，
要学会风雨中扬帆航行。
生活也不是不停地冲刺，
要根据情况适时调整。
不但要向着目标努力奋进，
也要看看左右将航标及时修正。
需要等待时沉着冷静，
需要前进时勇敢冲锋。
太累时不妨歇一歇，
太忙时可以缓一缓，

可以努力但不是拼命；
学会给生活留有空间，
你转身时才能灵活从容。

生活需一半烟火一半清欢，
人生需一半释然一半清醒。
生活中往往不如意事十之八九，
不可能事事收获、处处成功。
世上也没有永远的晴天和雨季，
要晴时晒太阳，雨时听雨声。
也许有风有雨的日子，
才承载了生活的厚重。

生活最美的不是风景，
是你快乐的心情。
不负光阴也不负自己，
繁忙的生活也需要步履轻盈。
以积极心态活出最佳状态，
便是面对生活的最好回应。
愿你懂得时刻热爱生活，
热爱才能感知生活的丰盈。

当你理解生活的多姿，
内心将多一份从容和淡定。
愿你珍惜每一个不期而遇，
愿你看淡每一个匿迹销声。
愿你把不易的生活过得有滋有味，
每天都有一个好的心情。

生活总是美好的，
一日三餐可以安享生活的平静，
奔波劳碌也能欣赏沿途的美景。
只要心中有阳光，
每天都会生机充盈；
只要心中有花香，
每个平淡的日子都有诗情。
过好每一个今天，
生活自然精彩纷呈；
过着自己喜欢的生活，
便是自己美好的人生。

去拥抱生活吧，
让今天过得充实，

让明天拥有愿景。

祈愿美好如约而至，

所有的坚持换来繁花似锦，

让我们共赴生活灿烂前程。

To Faraway (Group Poem)

Life

A person's life and living
Constitute a person's life.
Living is a combination of life and activities,
It not only requires your healthy body,
But also labor, movement, and action.
There is no easily obtained happy life in the world,
There is no simply achieved successful life either.
If you want to have the freedom to leave as you please,
You have to give up a lot of comfort and tranquility;
You want to receive a warm and sunny day, flowers and applause,

You have to move forward like a rock without fear of wind and rain.
If you treat life well, it will also give you gifts,
Which are hidden in your daily efforts.
All seemingly lucky things,
Are the result of accumulating strength.

Some people say that life is like the boiling water,
Regardless of whether it is hot or cold, as long as the temperature is appropriate;
Some people say that life is like taste,
Regardless of whether it's sour, sweet, bitter, or spicy, as long as it has a suitable taste;
Some people say that life is like a season,
Regardless of spring, summer, autumn, or winter, as long as you have the right mood.
In fact, whether one is willing to be lonely or not,
As long as you follow the principles that suit yourself.
Life does not need to be better than others,
But you need to excel every day compared to yourself in the past.

Everyone has dreams in life,
Because of them, you will take more action.
Perhaps reality cannot support dreams,

But dreams can support the rest of one's life.
Although dreams is a soft word,
As long as you believe, you can resist the hardness of reality.
Much of the time, beliefs determine the state of life,
In life, as long as dreams are still there,
Hard work will finally have another name Success.

The road of life is always rough,
As long as there is more understanding and composure,
In the dark days,
You can also see special scenery.
What can overcome difficulties is optimism and love,
Life is full of energy due to having a goal.
As long as there is love and dreams in the heart,
Life will get better and better.
There is no spring that cannot be welcomed,
There is no distance that cannot be reached,
As long as you keep moving towards your ideals.

Life won't always be smooth and calm,
Learn to sail in the wind and rain.
While life is not about constantly sprinting,
Adjust according to the situation in a timely manner.
We not only need to strive towards our goals,
Also, it is necessary to check the left and right navigation marks for timely correction.

When waiting, be calm and composed,
Be brave when you need to move forward.
When you're too tired, why not take a break,
When you're too busy, you can have a rest,
Working hard but not desperately;
Learn to leave space for your life,
Only when you turn around can you be flexible and composed.

Life requires half hustle and bustle as well as half calmness,
Life requires half relaxation and half clarity.
In life, things are often not as good as you wish,
It is impossible to reap and succeed everywhere.
There is no eternal sunny or rainy season in the world,
You can bask in the sun when it's sunny and listen to the sound of rain when it's raining.
Perhaps it is the windy and rainy days,
Which bear the weight of life.

The most beautiful thing in life is not the scenery,
But your happy mood.
Do not waste your time and be true to yourself,
A busy life also requires light steps.
Live the best state with a positive attitude,
It is the best situation to face life.
May you know how to love life at all times,

Only love can perceive the richness of life.
When you understand the diversity of life,
There will be more calmness and composure in the heart.
May you cherish every unexpected encounter,
May you overlook every disappearing sound.
May you live your difficult life with relish,
May you have a good mood every day.

Life is always beautiful——
Having three meals a day can make you enjoy a peaceful life,
You can enjoy the beautiful scenery along the way even if you work hard and run around.
As long as there is sunshine in the heart,
Every day will be full of vitality;
As long as there is the fragrance of flowers in the heart,
Every ordinary day has poetry.
As long as we live each day well,
Life is naturally colorful and exciting.
As long as you live the life you love,
It is the best life for yourself definitly.

Embrace life,
Let today be fulfilling,
Let tomorrow have a vision.
May good things come as promised.
May all persistence be rewarded with blooming flowers,
Let's go to the brilliant future of life together.

挫　折

花有花开花落，月有圆缺阴晴，
人生必有甜酸苦辣、挫折和成功。
生活不会时时厚待我们，
挫折和失误常常与我们同行。
福兮祸所伏——也许背后的阳光，
造成了你面前的阴影。
挫折能阻碍我们前进的速度，
却不能阻止我们拥有坚强的心灵。
不惧失败、内心乐观的人，
才会更接近幸福的人生。

人生就是一个磨炼的过程，
没有酸甜苦辣很难拥有成功。
没有鲜花要适应绿叶的芳香，
没有掌声要领悟独处的安静；
没有阳光要接受风雨的洗礼，
没有成功要看淡挫折的戏弄。
无论怎样的风风雨雨，
都要向着目标奋力前行。

只有一步一步攀登，
才会一点一点上升；
要脚踏实地、心往美景，
向更高山峰努力攀登。
成功固然可喜可贺，
失败也享受了一个过程。
这些坎坎坷坷的经历，
就是有滋有味的人生。

挫折和失败也是人生的部分，
孤独和懊悔必会不时伴行。
暂时的困顿坦然面对，
不妨多看看窗外的风景。
云雾终将会被大风吹散，
彩虹总是在风雨后横空。
只有经得起今天的沮丧，
才能收获明天的成功。

心有千千结不如遍种鲜花，
胸有万般怨不如盛满温情。
对于失去的不必留恋，

对于拥有的务必珍重。
挫折和失败已经成了过往，
不必过于放在心中。
请记住：你灰心了人生必然失色，
你笑了生活才能高兴。
要容得下日子的缺憾，
也要经得起人生的曲折和震动。
要以平常之心应对挫折，
太阳每天升起就是新的人生。

人生苦短、岁月易逝，
也许你还没有看清春夏的面容，
就已进入了生命的秋冬。
人生最好的时光永远是现在，
与其在挫折的阴霾中沉浸，
不如现在就开始行动；
与其在患得患失里焦虑，
不如在奋进中展示风情。
要不畏人情冷暖、命运坎坷，
对未来始终满怀希望和憧憬。

人生本来就很不容易，
不必处处在意别人的理解与认同。
走自己的路欣赏自己的风景，
学会在泪水中成长，汗水中前行。
挫折和失败并不可怕，
可怕的是失去信心和对目标的清醒。
人生路上都会有走过的弯路，
只要你不放弃就会走出泥泞。
把昨天的疼痛变成今天的动力，
奋力追赶明天的旭日东升。
请对自己说一声：
昨天已过，今天还行，明天会更行。

不要奢望人生有什么捷径，
不要期望轻而易举地成功。
谁都希望一生顺遂，
挫折后都有想要放弃甚至躺平。
但是不经过今天的奋斗和挫折，
就不可能看到明天的愿景。
一次华丽的跌倒胜过无数次徘徊，
一次失败也强于不敢行动。

我们要靠一次次的挫折和付出，
靠自己一步一个脚印地前行。
不付出比别人更多的努力，
怎能够获得想要的水到渠成。

人生无法一帆风顺，
却也不会永远波涛汹涌。
不管挫折对你怎样艰难，
人生总有属于你自己的春风。
只要迈开你的双脚，
就会走出自己的前程。
千帆竞过要学会坚韧不拔，
百舸争流要懂得坦然从容。
在做好每一件小事的积累当中，
迎接自己的柳暗花明；
在不羡慕谁也不依赖谁的努力中，
艰难跋涉攀登自己的山顶。
只要你尽心尽力去做，
即使不能如意也可以无憾终生。

向上的路总是难走的，

一定要百折不挠、持之以恒。
挫折没有那么多如果，
只有结果与后果共生。
没有谁可以生来自戴盔甲，
历练可以让自己具有耐力和本领。
错误和挫折教育了我们，
才使我们更加聪明。
克服自身缺点开拓新的领域，
在打磨自己中成长的历程，
也许是真正意义上的人生。

请记住，人生虽非一定要赢，
但不能输给过往的愚蠢和被动。
人不可能都成为英雄，
但是绝不能甘于平庸。
能力是成功的基石，
信心是关键的保证。
有时我们不是被挫折打败，
而是丧失信心造成。
过去形成现在、当下成就未来，
脚下的路就是将来的人生。

如果你想获得一个更好的未来，
当下的努力就是未来的黎明。
愿你不纠结过去也不畏惧未来，
把握好当下就是对挫折的回应。

一程一世界一步一风景，
请放飞自我、解放心灵。
愿你笑对挫折和失败，
掸去身上的泥土踏上新的征程。
行动不必在意时间的先后，
只有何时果断起程。
不管前方的路多么漫长，
要接近目标就要迈步前行。
每个努力的日子都在悄悄发芽，
它会在某一刻给你一个呆萌。
你若不辜负时光的美好，
它也一定不会辜负你的深情。
愿你跨过挫折再远征星辰大海，
归来依然光彩年轻。

Frustration

Flowers bloom and fall, and the moon waxes and wanes,
Life is bound to have ups and downs, setbacks, and successes.
Life does not always treat us well,
Frustrations and mistakes often accompany us.
Fortune and misfortune lurk—perhaps the sunshine behind,
Causes a shadow in front of you.
Although setbacks can hinder our progress,
They cannot prevent us from having a strong mind.
Only those optimistic people who are not afraid of failure,
Can get closer to a happy life.

Life is a process of refinement,
It is difficult to achieve success without experiencing the ups and downs, sweetness, bitterness, and spiciness.
Without flowers,one must adapt to the fragrance of green leaves,
Without applause, one must comprehend the tranquility of solitude;
Without sunshine, one must accept the baptism of wind and rain,
Learn to see light in the teasing of setbacks if you do not succeed.
No matter what kinds of winds and rains there are,
We must strive towards our goals.
Only through climbing step by step,
Can we gradually rise bit by bit;
We must be down—to—earth and focus on the beautiful scenery,

Strive to climb the higher peaks.
The final success is certainly congratulated,
Failure also brings a process of enjoyment.
These bumpy experiences
Constitute a meaningful life.

Setbacks and failures are also parts of life,
Loneliness and regret will accompany you from time to time.
Temporary difficulties should be faced calmly,
You can take a closer look at the scenery outside the window.
The clouds and mist will eventually be blown away by strong winds,
Rainbows always cross the sky after wind and rain.
Only by enduring today's frustration,
Can we reap tomorrow's success.

It's better to plant flowers everywhere than to have a thousand knots in the heart,
It is better to be filled with warmth than to have all kinds of grievances in the chest.
There is no need to dwell on what has been lost,
Be sure to cherish what you have owned.
Setbacks and failures have passed,
Do not put too much in your heart.
Please remember: if you lose heart, life will inevitably fade,
You can only be happy when you smile at life.
Tolerate the shortcomings of life,
Also withstand the twists and changes of life.

Deal with the ups and downs of the world with a calm heart,
The sun rises every day, bringing you a new life.

Life is short and time goes by,
Perhaps you have not seen the face of spring and summer clearly yet,
While you have already entered the autumn and winter of life.
The best time in life is always now,
Instead of immersing yourself in the haze of setbacks,
Take action now.
Instead of worrying about gains and losses,
Show your charm while striving forward.
Do not fear the ups and downs of fate,
Be always full of hope and longing for the future.

Life is inherently not easy,
There is no need to get others' understanding and identification for all things.
Take your own path and enjoy your own scenery,
Let us grow in tears and move forward in sweat.
Setbacks and failures are not terrible,
While losing confidence and explicit goals are more scarily.
There will always be detours on the road of life,
As long as you do not give up, you will get out of the mud.
Turn yesterday's pain into today's motivation,
Strive to catch up with tomorrow's rising sun.
Please tell yourself:
Yesterday has passed, today is okay, and tomorrow will be even better.

Do not expect any shortcuts in life,
Do not expect easy success.
Everyone hopes for a smooth life,
After setbacks, there will be a desire to give up or even lie down.
But without today's struggle and setbacks,
It is impossible to realize tomorrow's vision.
A magnificent fall is better than countless hesitations,
One failure is better than not daring to take action.
We must rely on our daily efforts, little by little,
Walk forward step by step on our own.
Without putting in more effort than others,
How can we get what we want naturally?

Life cannot be smooth sailing,
But it will not always be turbulent.
No matter how difficult setbacks may be for you,
Life always has its own spring breeze.
As long as you take steps forward,
You forge your own path ahead.
To compete with a thousand sails, you must learn to persevere,
A hundred boats competing for the flow should know How to be calm and composed.
Through the accumulation of well—tended small things,
You'll emerge from willow—shaded paths into sunlit blossoms.
Not envying anyone and not relying on anyone,
Struggle to climb your own mountaintop.
As long as you put in your best effort,
Even if things do not go as planned, you can live a lifetime without regrets.

The upward path is always difficult to take,
We must persevere.
There are not many "if onlys"for setbacks,
There are only outcomes and consequences co—occurring.
No one can be born wearing armor,
But experience can provide endurance and skills.
Errors and setbacks educate us,
Only then can we become smarter.
Overcoming our own shortcomings and exploring new fields,
The process of polishing one's own growth,
Perhaps is the true meaning of life.

Please remember, although life does not necessarily have to win,
But we cannot lose to the foolishness and passivity of the past.
People cannot all become heroes,
But we must not be content with mediocrity.
Ability is the cornerstone of success,
Confidence is the key gurantee.
Sometimes we are not defeated by difficulties,
But defeated by the loss of confidence.
The past forms the present, and the present creates the future,
The road underfoot is the future of life.
If you want to have a better future,
The current effort is the dawn of the future.
May you not dwell on the past or be afraid of future,
Grasping the present moment is a response to setbacks.

Every step brings a change of scene,
Please let yourself go and free your mind.
May you smile at setbacks and failures,
Bounce off the soil on your body and embark on a new journey.
Do not worry about the order of time in your actions,
Only consider that when to set off decisively matters.
No matter how long the road ahead might be,
To approach the goal, you must take steps forward.
Every day of hard work is quietly sprouting,
It will give you a silly and adorable moment.
If you do not let down the beauty of time,
It will definitely not disappoint your deep affection.
May you overcome setbacks and embark on an expedition to the stars and the sea,
When you return, wish you are still radiant and youthful.

低 谷

消沉常常会在挫折后出现，
美好也往往会在不经意间发生。
如果人生将你置于低谷，
也一定给你留下山上的白云青松。
与其悲观消沉不如乐观积极，
努力寻找出现转机的可能。

人人都会遇到低谷，
坚强的人总是不屈不挠努力拼争；
勇敢的人不会轻易放弃，
披荆斩棘把不能变成可能。
你不迈开走出低谷的脚步，
就不能到达最美的顶峰；
你不走出自我的阴影，
就不能开拓多彩的人生。
是的，只有经历过风雨兼程，
才能铸就自己的岁月峥嵘。

人生犹如旅途，

一时有一时的风雨，
一程也有一程的风景。
选择不同，道路必然不同，
不同的路就有不同的逆境。
路好不好走也许不能由你选择，
走不走却必须由你确定。
你前进，也许前程没有那么坎坷，
你放弃，一条坦途也会寸步难行。

请珍惜你的低谷时期，
它可以让你洞察事物的实情。
只有体验了岁月的悲欢离合，
才能看到人生的本质和真实面容。
这个世界上没有不受伤的人，
真正能够治愈自己的只能是自己，
不能依赖运气和别人的同情。
没有艰难哪里来的收获，
没有困顿哪里来的成功；
没有得失怎么会有选择，
没有痛苦怎么会有觉醒。
加油是制作美味的需要，

熬煎就是人生的必要过程。

这个世界有时会让你感觉寒冷，
但是只要你心中有热和爱，
必定会焐出温暖和光明。
你心若光明世界就不会黑暗，
你心怀希望就没有绝望的人生。
只要心中常驻诗和远方，
幸福快乐就会与我们同行。

你或许焦虑和迷惘，
但是请不要虚度人生。
不知道该做什么的时候，
不妨将你手中的事情清零；
不知道怎么开始的时候，
请把能做的事情做成。
有些事情也许我们无法改变，
但是可以换一种方式继续进行。
你努力了也许目标没有达到，
但躺平了必然是没有选择权的人生。

顺其自然是努力后的释然，
绝不是两手一摊的躺平。
只有蹚过心中的那道沟，
才敢逾越眼前的大坑；
只有迈过心中那道坎儿，
才能翻过面前的山峰。
只有用汗水去浇灌，
梦想才会柳绿花红。
没有到达不了的远方，
只要朝着目标努力前行。

如果你还有梦想，
就不必纠结回报是否丰盈。
要知道，你所浪费的今天，
是昨日逝者奢望的明天；
你所厌恶的现在，
是你未来回不去的曾经。
时间不会因你消沉而停下脚步，
我们必须善待自己的余生。
不管岁月如何难为了你，
都请你保持微笑和坚定。

默默耕耘、奋力前行，
去开拓属于自己的人生。

一天很长、一生很短，
转换的钥匙就在你的手中。
要把努力当成一种日常，
不能惧怕汗水和伤痛。
人人都有疲惫的时候，
愿你战胜惰性、重新调整；
让每个今天都优于昨天，
成功也许就在明天发生。

有时你与目标只有一步之遥，
这一步的代号就是意志坚定。
学习、思考、实践百折不挠，
胜不骄、败不馁、步履不停。
只有自信才能保持动力，
只有专注才能取得成功。
请把学习当成必需，
取得知识更在于运用。
勤于思考应对生活就会有智慧，

善于运用就会摆脱人生的平庸。

人生有时是自己与自己的斗争，
你能战胜自己就能获得成功。
不能管理好自己，
就会被外界战胜。
失意时不消沉是一种魄力，
得意时不忘形是一种智勇。
面对艰难困苦的淡定从容，
会扩展命运、丰富人生。
改变情绪和思维，
你将遇见未来更好的风景。

要成为自己命运的主导者，
就要独立思考不可追风。
要改变自己所处的困境，
就要认真分析三思而行。
世界上不仅敏锐聪慧才叫才能，
不为困难动摇、敢于面对失误，
才是做人最重要的本领。

人生就像一场马拉松，
让你跑得更久更远的是你的韧性。
请让努力成为一种习惯，
而不是杯水热度的三五分钟。
人生的收获很难一蹴而就，
成就往往出现在艰难的逆境。
想要的幸福很难易获得，
奋斗，命运才能掌握在自己手中。
逆风的方向也许更适合飞翔，
低谷时更需要努力攀登。
不能因为畏惧挫折而放弃希望，
不能因为担心路遥而止步不行。
愿你不负过往和未来，
绽放自己的独立和坚定。

奋斗真的很苦、前进真的很累，
能放弃吗？真的不能。
你不承担身边的人负担更重，
你不奋斗后代更需拼命。
鱼逆水而上、鸟逆风而行，
人不能惧怕岁月的朔风。

只有经过冰雪覆盖的冬天，
才会迎来鸟语花香的春景；
只有走过挥汗如雨的夏天，
才能获得秋天硕果累累的收成。
我们的汗水和逝去的青春，
将换来老人的安详、孩子的笑容。

人生的意义不仅仅在于成功，
也在不断探索未知的低谷之中。
努力打磨和塑造自己，
更能体会自己的价值和历程。
你的努力可能成功，
它会在某一刻成就你的人生；
你的努力也许不会成功，
但是你可以遇见自己多彩的人生。

人生没有十全十美，
不要苛求自己一定成功。
只要已经尽心尽力，
不妨向昨天的失败挥手辞行。
也不必迷茫于明天的不解，

要注重于今天的重新启程。
不妨放缓脚步多些耐心，
充实自我和内在的提升。
愿你经历一番严寒和酷暑，
依然对远方充满憧憬。

人生也是一场淬炼，
需守心克己、寡言勤行。
储存阳光以获取远方的鲜花，
心有温暖就不畏惧人生寒冷。
时间对所有人都公允平等，
努力会使人生每每不同。
努力会让你回首时问心无愧，
努力会让你更加接近愿景。
与他人的差距在于你的努力，
未来的样子由你现在决定。

一天很长、一生很短，
转换的钥匙就在手中。
要把努力当成一种日常，
不能惧怕汗水和伤痛。

人人都有疲惫的时候，
愿你克服惰性、步履不停。
只要让每个今天都优于昨天，
成功也许就在明天发生。

漫漫人生我们都会遇到低谷，
你把它当成鸿沟它就是万丈深坑；
如果把它当成机遇，
它下面必会潜藏着命运的公平。
每个人都有自己的光点，
要把未来的道路走稳踏平。
别高估了困难的实力，
也不要低估自己的能力和行动。
你若懦弱人生必然风雨飘摇，
你若坚强生活就不会沉重。
只有抛弃消极努力奋起，
才能把困境变成愿景。

梅花穿越了风雪苦寒，
才有芳香四溢、凌傲严冬。
人经历过波折低谷，

才能遇事举重若轻、从容淡定。
征服过悬崖峭壁，
才能履险如夷欣赏高峰的美景；
心胸似海宽阔，
才能放下过去装入未来的日程。
请多一点自信、智慧和勇气，
朝着理想的方向努力前行。

时光因多彩而美丽，
岁月因悠久而厚重。
人生是一次充满未知的跋涉，
一定不要迷惑于眼前的困境。
迈开步，路就在脚下延伸，
挺起胸，别人未必高你一等。
以积极的态度面对生活，
是面对低谷应有的心胸。

低谷是大海的一个波涛，
终将归于平静；
低谷是天空的一片阴云，
总要雨过天晴。

理想的种子需要你去播撒，
事业的荒原需要你去耕种，
生活的画卷需要你去描绘，
雕塑自己需要一锤一凿刻成。
愿你道路艰辛依然一往无前，
对未来与生活充满希望和激情。

请相信，在人生的航道上，
你只要扬帆总会有八面来风；
那些艰苦的拼搏，
终会像星光照亮你的航程。
愿你不气馁不松懈走出低谷，
策马扬鞭奔赴你想要的远景。

Low Ebb

Low mood often appears after setbacks,
While wonderful things often happen unintentionally.
If life puts you at a low point,

It will definitely also leave you the white clouds and green pines on the mountain.
It's better to be optimistic and positive than pessimistic and depressed,
Strive to find the possibility of a turning point.

Everyone will encounter the low point,
Strong people always persevere and strive to compete;
Brave people never give up easily,
Overcome obstacles to turn the impossible into the possible.
If you do not take steps out of the trough,
You cannot reach the most beautiful peak;
If you do not step out of your own shadow,
You cannot explore a colorful life.
Yes, only after experiencing storms and hardships,
Can you build your own extraordinary world.

Life is like a journey,
Wind and storms appear at different times,
Every journey has its own scenery.
Different choices inevitably lead to different paths,
Different paths lead to different adversities.
Whether the road is easy or not may not be up to you to choose,
Whether to go or not must be determined by you.
You may not have such a bumpy future if you

move forward,
If you give up, even a smooth path becomes difficult for you to more.

Please cherish your low period,
It can give you insight into the truth of things.
Only by experiencing the joys and sorrows of time,
Can you see through the essence and truth of life.
There is no one in this world who would not be hurt,
The only one who can truly heal yourself is you,
You cannot rely on luck and sympathy from others.
Where does the harvest come from without difficulties?
Where does success come from without frustrations?
How can there be a choice without gains and losses?
How can there be arousal without pain?
Oil is necessary in making delicious food,
Boiling is the necessary process in life.

This world sometimes makes you feel cold,
But as long as you have warmth and love in your heart,
You will surely get warmth and light.
If your heart is bright, the world would not be dark,
If you hold hope in your heart, there would be no desperate life.
As long as poetry and distant places remain in your heart,
Happiness and joy will accompany you.

You may be anxious and confused,
But please do not waste your life.
When you do not know what to do,
You may as well put the things in your hands aside;
When you do not know how to start,
Please do what you can do.
There are some things that we may not be able to change,
But we can continue in a different way.
You may have tried hard but not achieved your goal,
But lying down is inevitably a life without choice.

The so—called letting nature take its course is the release after working hard,
It is not lying with both hands spreading out.
Only crossing the ditch in your heart,
Then can you dare to cross the big pit in front of you;
Only crossing the hurdle in your heart,
Then can you climb over the mountain peak in front of you.
Only watering with sweat,
Can dreams bring green willows and red flowers.
There is no distant place that cannot be reached,
Just strive towards the goal.

If you still have dreams,
There is no need to worry about whether the returns are abundant.

You should know, the day you wasted today,
Is the tomorrow that the deceased hoped for yesterday;
What you detest now,
Is the past that you can not go back to in the future.
Time will not stop because of your depression,
We must treat ourselves well for the rest of the lives.
No matter how difficult times may be,
Please keep smiling and be firm.
Silently cultivate and strive forward,
To explore your own life.

A day is long, while a lifetime is short,
The key to conversion is in your hands.
Make effort a daily routine,
Cannot fear sweat and pain.
Everyone has moments of exhaustion,
May you overcome laziness and retune.
Make every today better than yesterday,
Success may happen tomorrow.

Sometimes you are only one step away from your goal,
The code for this step is firm will.
Perseverance in learning, thinking, and practicing,
Do not be arrogant in victory, or discouraged in defeat,
and keep moving forward.
Only confidence can maintain motivation,
Only by focusing can success be achieved.
Please treat learning as a necessity,

Getting knowledge is aimed to apply it.
Being diligent in thinking and living will bring you wisdom,
Being good at using it will help you get rid of the mediocrity of life.

Life is sometimes a struggle with yourself,
You can achieve success by defeating yourself.
If you cannot manage yourself well,
You will be defeated by the outside world.
Not being depressed when feeling down is a kind of courage,
Not forgetting oneself when feeling proud is a kind of wisdom and courage.
Facing difficulties with calmness and composure,
You will expand and enrich your life.
Change your mind and thinking,
You will encounter better scenery in the future.

To become the master of your own destiny,
You must think independently and not follow the trend.
To change the predicament you are in,
You need to carefully analyze and think before taking action.
In the world, not only sensitivity and intelligence are called talents,
Not wavering in face of difficulties, daring to face

mistakes,
are a person's most important skills.

Life is like a marathon,
What makes you run longer and farther is your resilience.
Please make effort a habit,
Instead of being like three minutes of water heat.
The harvest of life is difficult to achieve at once,
Achievements often arise in difficult adversity.
The happiness one desires is rarely easy,
Struggle is the key to mastering one's destiny.
The direction against the wind may be more suitable for flying,
We need to work harder for climbing during the low periods.
We cannot give up hope out of setbacks fearing,
We cannot stop because of worrying about the distance.
May you live up to your past and future,
Be independent and firm.

Struggling is really hard, also moving forward is really tiring,
Can we give up? Of course not.
If you do not bear, the burden of those people's around you will be heavier,
If you do not strive, future generations need to work harder.
Fish go up against the water, birds go against the wind,
People cannot fear the cold wind of time.
Only after ice—and—snow covered winter,
Will we welcome the spring scenery of birds singing and

flowers blooming;
Only through the sweat drenched summer,
Can we obtain a bountiful harvest in autumn.
Our sweat and lost youth,
Will bring peace to the elderly and smiles to the children.

The meaning of life is not only about success,
But also constantly exploring the unknown future.
Strive to polish and shape yourself,
You will understand better your own value and journey.
You may succeed through efforts,
It will accomplish your life at some time;
You may fail after so many efforts have been made,
But you can encounter your own colorful life.

Life is never perfect,
Do not make excessive demands that you must success.
As long as you have done your best,
Why not wave goodbye to yesterday's failure?
Do not be lost in tomorrow's confusion either,
Focus on today's starting afresh.
Try to slow down and be more patient,
Enrich yourself and enhance your inner world.
May you experience both cold and hot,
Still eagerly long for the distance.

Life is also a process of tempering,
Be mindful and self—restrained, be quiet and diligent in action.

Store sunlight to obtain flowers from afar,
If there is warmth in heart, one will not fear the coldness of life.
Time is fair to everyone,
Working hard, will always make life different.
Effort will make you look back with a clear conscience,
Effort will bring you closer to your vision.
The difference between you and others depends on your efforts,
The future is up to you to decide now.

A day may be long, while a lifetime may be short,
The key to conversion is in your hands.
Make effort a daily routine,
Do not fear sweat and pain.
Everyone experiences the moments of exhaustion,
May you overcome laziness and keep moving forward.
As long as every today is better than yesterday,
Success may happen tomorrow.

In the long journey of life, you will all encounter lows,
If you treat it as a chasm, it is a bottomless pit;
If you treat it as an opportunity,
Underneath it lies the fairness of fate definitely.
Everyone has his/her own bright spot,
Pave steadily the way for the future.
Do not overestimate the strength of difficulties,
Do not underestimate your own abilities and actions.

If you are weak, life will inevitably be full of difficulties,
If you are strong, life will not be too heavy.
Only by abandoning negative efforts and rising up,
Can you turn difficulties into visions.

Plum blossoms have weathered the wind and snow,
Only then they gain fragrance and stand proundly in the fierce winter.
People have experienced ups and downs,
Only then they are able to handle situations with ease and composure.
Allowing conquered steep cliffs,
People can walk through danger and appreciate the beautiful scenery of the peak;
The heart is as broad as the sea,
People can let go of the past and put the future agenda into it.
Please have more confidence, wisdom, and courage,
Strive towards the ideal direction.

Time is beautiful because of its colors,
Time is thick for it is endless.
Life is a journey full of unknowns,
Never be confused by the current predicament.
Keep moving, the road stretches underfoot,
Stand up straight, others may not necessarily be superior to you.
Facing life with a positive attitude

Is the required breadth of mind that one should have when facing adversity.

The low ebb is a wave of the sea,
Which will eventually return to peace;
The low ebb is a cloud in the sky,
It will always clear up after the rain.
The ideal seeds need you to sow,
The wilderness of your career requires you to cultivate,
The painting of life requires you to depict,
Sculpting yourself needs to be done with a hammer and chisel.
May you continue to forge ahead despite the hardships of your journey,
Full of hope and passion for the future and life.

Please believe that on the path of life,
As long as you set sail, there will always be winds from all directions;
Those arduous struggles
will eventually illuminate your voyage like starlight.
May you not be discouraged or slack off, and walk out of the trough,
Ride your horse and whip towards the distant view you desire.

烦　恼

人人都会有烦恼，
谁都会遇到麻烦的事情。
请你充满希望和热情，
少些抱怨、多些行动。

人生是把汗水换成柴米油盐，
做出酸甜苦辣百味的过程。
这些各种滋味的生活经历，
在装点着我们心中的大海星空。

这个世界有许多的不足和未知，
人生有许多的无奈和伤痛。
无法改变的东西应当舍弃，
这并不是你的过错和无能。

万事不可能总是如意，
要拿得起放得下。
不能如愿的选择释然，
不能得到的坦然从容。

该放下的要有悠然见南山的淡定，
无法挽回要有千金去复来的豪情。
面对各种烦恼和沮丧，
耿耿于怀不如把忧愁清零。

麻烦的事情也许不会把你压垮，
情绪却可以将你坠入黑洞。
你可以有选择地发泄烦恼，
更要学会对情绪的管控。

顺利时要多一份思索，
困难时要多一份淡定；
成功时要多一份低调，
失落时要多一份从容。

不盲目攀比也不纠结过往，
不斤斤计较也不孤芳自赏。
当你一点一点学会克制自己，
你就学会了驾驭自己的人生。

无论何时都要宽慰自己，

把开心变成一种动能。
不管身在何处、年龄几许，
都别让烦恼遮盖了你的身影。

请谨记：冲动是魔鬼，
烦恼时切不可以冲动。
不要因为一时的失去理智，
造成无可挽回的后悔终生。

烦恼不仅是身体的劳累，
内心的熬煎更为严重。
面对困难一笑而过那是大度，
面对烦恼一笑而过就是聪明。

微笑有时比语言更有力量，
温暖了他人也改善了自己的环境。
心有阳光一切皆会灿烂，
脚踏实地才能更上楼层。

命运不会任由你摆布放纵，
它像蒲公英一样看似自由实则随风。

唯有摆脱他人眼光的牢笼，
你才能遇见自己广阔的前景。

面对复杂的世界，
抛弃那些无关紧要的繁庸。
当你跳出不切实际的圈子，
生活自然呈现简单清静。

虽然前进一步可有美丽风景，
后退一步却可获得平淡心境。
日子未必都要红红火火，
但是一定要和睦安宁。

人的一生会遇到 2920 多万人，
擦肩过后只有少数人陪你一生。
每个人的认知和能力各不一样，
每个人的人生轨迹也不尽相同。

与优秀的人同行可以走得更远，
与懂你的人相处就不辜负此生。
遇到想不通的事情请做换位思考，

对待世间一些事物要心存包容。

人人都有自己的个性，
需要相互谦让和尊重。
对他人的谦让就是对自己的尊重，
我们都活在体验人生的过程之中。

你以为的仅仅是所认为的以为，
它不是现实剧目的真实场景。
暂时接受不了的不要急于否定，
要等一等我们认知的修正。

人不怕无知只怕固执，
自以为是的结果只能是伤痛。
我们必须处处探索周边环境，
我们需时时与他人加强沟通。

其实一切的烦恼都是自找，
你若放下便是心绪的安平。
只有学会发现生活的美好，
才能拥有幸福快乐的人生。

请丢掉昨日烦恼拥抱今日平静，
对明天的美好一往情深。
当下风云多变的平淡生活，
更需倍加珍惜尽享景明。

要明白，痛和苦也是一笔人生财富，
它会铺垫和踏实你未来的路程。
请用智慧去面对所有的烦恼，
请用微笑接纳不如意的事情。

不要留恋过去的辉煌，
不要计较收获不如付出丰盈。
好事坏事都会成为追忆的往事，
大事小事都将是茶余饭后的笑声。

人生比烦恼更懊恼的事情，
或许是竹篮打水一场空。
一个人有了健康才有正常的生活，
失去这个其他所有只能是零。

与其将时间浪费在无聊的人和事，

不如将自己给予读书睡觉和运动；
只要有益于身心健康和生活，
也不妨给予山河草木与花鸟鱼虫。

未来请你好好珍惜自己，
关照自己的一饭一羹。

人生烦恼你要开心生活，
日子无趣你要自己找乐，
生活苦涩你要善于调味，
茫茫大海需自己摆渡航行。

无论生活给你有多少考验，
过好当下是对生活最好的回应。
无论世界对你有多少误解，
明天醒来太阳依然东升。

请保持爱心笑看人生悲喜，
不必在意得失虚名；
也不必畏惧人间生死磨难，
乐对一切烦恼与病痛。

以平常之心看待人间冷暖，
以平淡之心对待世事纷争，
以平静之心处理身边事务，
更要用平和之心善待人生。

放下烦恼腾出手来拥抱生活吧，
学会轻装前进不必捶胸顿足。
请每天绽放笑容迎接新的一天，
沿着前行的足迹欣赏沿途的风景。

每天的太阳都有温暖，
每天的醒来都是新生。
请丢掉以前的一切烦恼，
拥抱以后的每一分钟。

愿你把开心变成习惯，
面对生活乐观而坚定。
请用微笑面对烦恼，
你会拥有不一样的人生。

Annoyance

Actually, everyone will have troubles,
Everyone will encounter trouble.
May you be filled with hope and passion,
Complain less, act more.

Life is a process of exchanging sweat for firewood, rice, oil, and salt,
And making sour, sweet, bitter, and spicy flavors.
These various flavors of life experiences
Adorn the sea and starry sky in our hearts.

There are many shortcomings and unknowns in this world,
There is much helplessness and pain in life.
Something that cannot be changed should be discarded,
This is not your fault or incompetence.

Everything cannot always go smoothly,
Take it easy.
Let go those choices that can not be achieved.
Be calm and composed for those that can not obtain.

Be placid and leisurely as if seeing the South Mountain for those that should be put down.

Be generous and optimistic for those that can not be retrieved.
Life inevitably faces various troubles and frustrations,
It's better to eliminate worries than to dwell on them.

Troubles may not crush you,
But emotions can plunge you into a black hole.
You can choose to vent your troubles,
But it is even more important to learn how to control emotions.

When things go smoothly, we need to think more,
Be more calm when facing difficulties;
When getting success, one should keep a low profile,
When feeling lost, one should have more composure.

Not blindly compare or dwell on the past,
Be not petty or aloof.
As you gradually learn to restrain yourself,
You will learn to control your own life.

Always comfort yourself,
Turn happiness into a driving force.
No matter where you are or how old you are,
Do not let worries cover up your figure.

Please remember: impulsiveness is the devil,
Do not act impulsively when you are troubled.

Do not lose your sanity for a moment,
Or it will cause irreparable regret for life.

Fatigue is not just physical exertion,
The inner torment is even more severe.
Facing difficulties with a smile is magnanimous,
Smiling away troubles is smart.

Smiling is sometimes more powerful than words,
Being warm to others is to improve your own environment.
With sunshine in the heart, everything will shine brightly,
Being down—to—earth can lead to higher floors.

Fate will not be at your mercy and indulgence,
It looks like a dandelion, seemingly free but actually following the wind.
Only by breaking free from the cage of others' eyes,
Can you reach your own broad prospects.

Facing a complex world,
You should abandon those trivial matters.
When you jump out of unrealistic circles,
Life naturally presents simplicity and tranquility.

Indeed, taking a step forward can bring beautiful scenery,
Taking a step back can lead to a calm state of mind.
Life does not necessarily have to be bright and lively,
But it must be harmonious and peaceful.

In a person's lifetime, he or she will encounter over 29.2 million people,
After passing by so many people, only a few will accompany you for a lifetime.
Everyone's cognition and abilities are different,
Everyone's life trajectory is different as well.

Walking with excellent people can go further,
Getting along with people who understand you will not disappoint your life.
When encountering things that you cannot understand, please put yourself in the shoes,
Be tolerant towards some things in the world.

People have their own personality,
Mutual humility and respect are required.
Respect for others is respect for yourself,
We all live in the process of experiencing life.

What you think is just what you think,
It is not a real scene in a reality.
Do not rush to deny what you cannot accept temporarily,
We have to wait for the correction of our cognition.

It is not afraid of ignorance, but stubbornness should be paid attention to,
The result of self—righteousness can only be pain.
We must explore the surrounding environment

everywhere,
We also need to constantly strengthen communication with others.

In fact, all troubles are self—inflicted,
Let it go, it will bring peace to your mind.
Only by learning to discover the beauty of life,
Can we have a happy and fulfilling life.

Please let go of yesterday's troubles and embrace today's simplicity,
Deeply cherish the beauty of tomorrow.
The current ever—changing and mundane life,
Need to be cherished and enjoy the scenery even more.

Try to understand, pain and suffering are also a wealth of life,
It will lay the foundation and secure your future journey.
Please face all your troubles with wisdom,
Please accept unpleasant things with a smile.

Do not dwell on the past glory,
Do not worry that rewards are not as abundant as efforts.
Good or bad things will all become memories of the past,
Both big and small things will be laughter after meals.

The things in life that are more regretful than troubles
is an empty bamboo basket.

A person can only live a normal life with good health,
Without health everything else would be nothing.

Instead of wasting time on boring people and things,
Dedicating yourself to reading, sleeping, and exercising;
As long as it is beneficial for physical and mental health in daily life,
Why not enjoy scenery such as mountains, rivers, plants, flowers, birds, fish, and insects?

Please cherish yourself well in the future,
Three meals a day, eat well and keep healthy.

You should live happily amidst the troubles of life,
You should find delights by yourself in simple and ordinary life,
You should be good at seasoning the bitterness of life,
You should navigate your voyage in the vast ocean.

No matter how many tests life has given you,
Living well in present is the best response to life.
No matter how many misunderstandings the world has about you,
Tomorrow when you wake up, the sun will still rise in the east.

Please maintain a loving smile and witness the joys and sorrows of life,

Do not worry about gains and losses or fame;
There is no need to fear the hardships of life and death in this world,
Enjoy all troubles and pains.

Try to view the warmth and coldness of the world with a calm heart,
Treat worldly disputes with a calm heart,
Handle affairs around you with a calm heart,
Treat life with a peaceful heart.

Let go of your troubles and free up your hands to embrace life,
Learn to move forward lightly without pounding your chest.
Please smile every day to welcome a new day,
Appreciate the scenery along the journey.

The sun is warm every day,
Waking up every day is a rebirth.
Please let go of all past troubles,
Embrace every minute in the rest of your life.

May you turn happiness into a habit,
Facing life with optimism and determination.
Please face your troubles with a smile,
You will have a different life.

成　功

人生最幸福的事情，
是把梦想变成了现实。
但它不会在舒适和愉悦里产生，
成功诞生于痛苦和汗水之中。
不要幻想不劳而获的幸福，
不要相信信手拈来的成功。
人生的画图需要自己描绘，
一笔一画勾勒才有灿烂美景。

成功者并不都是天赋异禀，
是在日常中打造出别样的风景。
优秀者的卓越也不会天生，
那是艰难困苦磨炼而成。
只要日复一日的努力，
你也会收获穿石的一点一滴，
成就一个不一样的人生。

一个人经过不同程度的磨炼，
会有不同程度的素养和文明。

美酒越封藏味道越醇厚，
芝麻越挤压滋味越香浓。
经过风风雨雨各种磨难，
是你成功的最好证明。
只有经过岁月的艰辛与繁华，
才能在沧海桑田中拓出一片人生。

不要短期得不到回报就放弃努力，
每一点付出都会是路上的明灯。
为了不与自己的成功失之交臂，
必须努力奔跑而不是为让别人感动。
我们不清楚成功需要奔跑多久，
也不知道前面还有多长的路程；
只要认真生活、迈步前行，
就是最好的解题和充实的人生。

成功是一次次努力的积累，
绝不是一夜降临的梦寐和慵懒。
收获也不会都来自巧合，
必须用日复一日的付出摆平。
不怕你每天迈的步子太小，

只怕你停下脚步不再前行；
不怕你每天做事太少，
只怕你无所事事碌碌无用。
每日一点一滴的雕刻，
终会把自己塑造得与众不同。

成功不要期望一蹴而就，
梦想也不必急于求成。
长路漫漫前行则心无旁骛，
岁月悠悠驻足则波澜不惊。
要把平凡的事业做得非凡，
要把普通的工作干得出众。
别把所有希望都寄托在明天，
只有努力每一个今天，
明天才会更加光明。

没有唾手可得的成功，
也没有不战而成的英雄。
你要想看到更美的高峰，
就要让高峰先看到你的攀登。
成功的道路虽有坎坷和荆棘，

主动权却掌握在自己手中。
不管前路多么崎岖泥泞，
只要方向正确就须奋力前行。
努力也许一时不会开花结果，
但是每次努力会更接近成功。

成功没有什么诀窍，
提高自己、协同别人就会优化环境。
守住原则成功就会少一些迷茫，
懂得感恩努力就会多一些动能；
坚持学习必然自我增值，
改变思维必将拓展格局和心灵。
学会控制自己就控制了生活，
掌握了生活也是人生的成功。

世上最好的保鲜方式是不断进步，
普通的改变将改变普通。
把简单的事情做对就不简单，
把平常的事情做好就不平庸。
只会幻想而不行动的人，
必然看不到收获果实的美景。

再小的坚持也是努力，
愿你在坚持中迎来一个个成功。

成功可喜，它鼓舞大家的情绪；
成功可贺，它完成了对你的提升。
但是切不可被胜利所麻痹，
一定要时时保持头脑清醒。
成功不一定能成为永恒成就，
它也不是凭借你一人的神勇。
许多客观条件和众人的支持，
是你成功的绿叶。

成功者很少受到指责，
我们自己却要有必须的理性。
不能沉浸在鲜花和掌声之中。
要多找存在的不足和失误，
要多听不同的措施和心声。
庆功的美酒固然香浓陶醉，
为了未来，不如细品苦涩的茗茶。

你可以成为自己的太阳，

无需凭借别人的光芒和人情。
但是有才智也需要气和心平，
有成就更需谦虚谨慎、义正言明。
在拥有无限可能的岁月里，
可以坚持和努力追逐心中的美梦；
但是只有在众人的支持和点赞中，
你才能真正体会到收获和成功。

成功了也须保持谦恭的态度，
要记得，你并不比别人高出一等。
一定要继续前进，
目标就是下一个更高的山峰。
一时一事的成功并不伟大，
个人的成就惠及了人民大众，
历史才会把个人记在心中。

要到达最美的远方，
必须继续大步前行，
不要沉醉在成功的荣誉之中。
人生的成功不仅在于收获，
更在于贡献和播种。

要明白，个人众多的成功，
不如科技和社会的一点成功。
个人的成就也许微不足道，
造福人民的业绩才会彪炳史册。

人最大成功也许不是财富和才能，
而是你的善良和真诚。
要懂得同则亲、异则敬，
不拿自己的尺子丈量别人的人生。
每个人的看法和想法不尽相同，
因为每个人都长着自己的眼睛。
依靠脱离实际的教条和经验，
会给我们带来巨大的苦痛；
必须根据变化的现实适时调整，
历史的教训就是我们的警钟。

目标植于内心，
能力源于行动。
前进需要一步一个脚印，
努力需要一点一滴持之以恒。
那一锤一凿打磨自己的过程，

必然伴随着汗水和光荣。
我们不是仅仅为了成功而去努力，
努力是为制作一个有意义的成功。

成功者都是优秀和幸运的，
每一个成功者都是英雄。
英雄的出处来自内心的强大，
来自对梦想的执著和憧憬；
来自对事业的坚持与踏实，
来自面对浮华的不屑与淡定。
平凡的人努力做好平凡的事，
每个平凡的人都可以成为英雄。
愿你束之高阁荣誉和光环，
再接再厉收获岁月新的成功。

Success

The happiest thing in life
is turning dreams into success.

But it will not occur in comfort and pleasure,
Success is born from pain and sweat.
Don't fantasize about obtaining happiness without effort,
Do not believe in easy success.
The painting of life needs to be drawn by yourself,
A magnificent scenery can only be sketched stroke by stroke.

Successful people are not all gifted,
Create unique landscapes in daily life.
The excellence of distinguished people is not innate,
That is the result of hardships and trials.
As long as you work hard day after day,
You will also reap every little bit of stone penetration,
Achieve a different life.

A person who has undergone varying degrees of refinement,
will have varying degrees of literacy and civilization.
The more wine is sealed, the richer its flavor becomes,
The more squeezed sesame seeds are, the more fragrant and rich their flavor becomes.
Only through wind, rain, and various hardships,
Can your success be proved.
Only through the hardships and prosperity of life,
Can you create a colorful life.

Don't give up without short—term returns,
Every little effort will be a light on the road.
In order to not miss success,
You must strive to run, not to move others.
We do not know how long we need to run,
And how long the journey ahead is.
But as long as we live seriously and move forward,
We have the best solution and a fulfilling life.

Success is the accumulation of repeated efforts,
It is not a dream or laziness that comes overnight.
The harvest will not all come from coincidence,
It must be balanced with daily efforts.
Not afraid that you take too small steps every day,
I'm only afraid you'll stop moving forward.
Not afraid that you do too few things every day,
I'm only afraid you'll be idle and useless.
Every day, make efforts little by little,
You will eventually shape yourself into someone unique.

Do not expect to be successful overnight,
Dreams do not have to be rushed to achieve.
The long road ahead is full of distractions,
When time passes by, the waves remain calm.
Make ordinary endeavors extraordinary,
Do not pin all your hopes on tomorrow,
Strive every day,
Tomorrow will be even brighter.

There is no easy success,
There is no hero who becomes heroic without fighting.
If you want to see a more beautiful peak,
You should let the peaks see your climbing.
The road to success may be bumpy and thorny,
The initiative is in your own hands.
No matter how rugged and muddy the road ahead might be,
As long as the direction is correct, you must strive forward.
Effort may not bear fruit for a while,
But every effort is definitely closer to success.

There is no shortcut to success,
Improving yourself and collaborating with others will optimize the environment.
By adhering to principles, you will experience less confusion,
Knowing how to be grateful will give you more inner energy;
Persistent study will inevitably lead to self—improvement,
Developing your mindset will inevitably expand your perspective and soul.
Learning to control yourself means controlling life,
Controlling life is the success of life.

The best way to preserve freshness in the world is to constantly improve,
Ordinary changes will change ordinary things.
Doing simple things right is not easy,
Doing ordinary things well is not mediocre.
People who only fantasize without taking action,
Would not be able to see the beautiful scenery of harvest.
Even the smallest persistence is effort,
May you achieve success one by one through persistence.

Success is gratifying, because it inspires everyone's emotions,
Success is praiseworthy, because it has completed the improvement for you.
But we must not be complacent by victory,
Always maintain a clear mind.
Success may not necessarily become an eternal achievement,
It does not rely solely on your courage.
Many objective conditions and the support from the public are the green leaf of your success.

Successful individuals will not be blamed,
We need to have the necessary rationality.
Cannot be immersed in flowers and applause.
We need to identify more shortcomings and mistakes,
Listen to different measures and more voices.

The celebratory wine is unquestionably rich and intoxicating,
For the future, it's better to savor the bitter tea.

You can become your own sun,
No need to rely on other people's radiance and favor.
But having intelligence also requires calmness of mind,
To achieve success, must be humble, cautious, and speak with righteousness.
In the years of infinite possibilities,
You can persist and strive to pursue the dreams of your heart;
But only with the support and likes of others,
Can you truly experience the harvest and success.

Even if you succeed, you need to maintain a humble attitude,
Remember, you are not superior to others.
You must be in a state of continuous progress,
The goal is to reach the next higher mountain peak.
It should be noted that the success of a moment or thing is not great,
Personal achievements have benefited the general public,
History will remember individuals in their hearts.

To reach the most beautiful distant place,
We must continue to take big strides forward.

Please do not indulge in the glory of success,
The success of life lies not only in the harvest,
But also, it lies in contribution and sowing.
We should understand that numerous personal success is not as successful as technology and society.
Personal achievements may be insignificant,
Only achievements that benefit the people will shine through the ages.

The greatest success of a person may not be wealth and talent,
But kindness and sincerity.
We should understand that similarities lead to kinship, while differences lead to respect,
Do not measure others' lives with your ruler.
Different people have different opinions and ideas,
Because everyone has his or her own eyes.
Relying on dogmas and experiences that are detached from reality,
Will bring us great pain;
We must adjust in a timely manner according to the changing reality,
The lessons of history are our alarm bells.

The goal is rooted in the heart,
Ability comes from action.
Moving forward requires taking it a step and a day at a time,

Effort requires perseverance bit by bit.
The process of carving yourself with each hammer and chisel,
Will inevitably be accompanied by sweat and glory.
We cannot strive solely for success,
Effort is to create a meaningful success.

Yes, successful people are excellent and lucky,
Every successful person is a hero.
The origin of heroes comes from their inner strength,
From the persistent pursuit and longing for dreams;
From persistence and steadfastness in one's profession,
From disdain and calmness in the face of extravagance.
Ordinary people strive to do ordinary things well,
Every ordinary person can become a hero.
May you set aside your lofty honor and halo,
Keep up the good work and reap new successes in the years ahead.

尾 声

生命的旅程是那么的长，
长到无数个轮回的春夏秋冬；
它又是那么的短，
短到一眨眼仿佛一世匆匆。

人生在世也许是为了经历和尝试，
经过越多心神就会更加平静。
对待人和事物的判断更加客观，
遭遇不平和坎坷会越发从容。

要明白：做人不一定要风风光光，
但是一定要堂堂正正。
做事不一定要尽善尽美，
但是一定要尽其所能。

不必自卑和羡慕别人，
每个人都有自己绚丽的天空。
让我们始终保持心有所爱与勇气，
不管已经处于什么情境。

生命因珍惜而灿烂，
生活因平淡而温情。
自己喜欢的日子就是最好的生活，
成为更好的自己就是最好的人生。

相信暂时的静默是为了永久的繁荣，
暂时的离别是为了更好的重逢。
相信一切的一切都会过去，
请耐心等待，黑夜过后必将迎来黎明。

愿抛撒绿色的橄榄枝，
愿吉祥的白鸽自由飞翔，
让战争的硝烟不再弥空。

愿你安好，我无恙，
让我们彼此康宁。
愿你历尽风雨心中依然滚烫，
挥别过往，生活事业皆有所成。

让我们的内心更加宽阔吧，
这笔财富将惠及我们的一生。

让我们相互勉励和隔空拥抱吧，
也许你我就在你我的心中。

此时已是金风阵阵、皓月当空，
露白今夜又见点点晶莹；
鸟鸣果香犹如思绪绵绵，
远方的你啊，还望多多珍重……

Epilogue

The journey of life is so long,
Because of countless cycles of spring, summer, autumn, and winter;
But it is also so short,
In the blink of an eye, it feels like a fleeting life.

Life may be for experiencing and trying,

The more you try, the calmer your mind will be.
If you make more objective judgments about people and things,
When encountering hardships and obstacles you will become calmer and more composed.

Try to understand: being a person does not necessarily have to be glamorous,
But it must be dignified and upright.
Doing things does not necessarily have to be perfect,
But you must do your best.

There is no need to feel inferior to or envious of others,
Everyone has his or her own brilliant sky.
Let us always maintain love and courage in our hearts,
No matter what situation you are already in.

Life shines brightly because it is cherished,
Life is warm because of the ordinary days.
The day you like is the best life,
Becoming a better self is the best life.

I believe that temporary silence is for permanent prosperity,
Temporary separation is for a better reunion.
Believe that everything will pass,
Please be patient, after the dark night comes the

dawn.

May I scatter green olive branches,
May the auspicious white dove fly freely,
Let the smoke of war no longer happen.

May you be well, I am safe and sound,
Let's have peace and health with each other.
May your heart stay hot despite the wind and rain,
Farewell to the past, both life and career have achieved success.

Let's broaden our hearts,
This wealth will benefit us for the rest of our lives.
Let's encourage and embrace each other from afar,
Perhaps you and I are in our hearts.

At this moment, the golden wind is blowing and the bright moon is in the sky,
Tonight, the dew glistens white – a thousand crystal drops, seen once more;
The chirping of birds and the fruity aroma are like endless thoughts,
You in the distance, I hope you take care of yourself more.

TAX 自白

我就是税，
TAX 是我，
我是法绳，
我是玉帛，
我是贡献……
不，我就是我。

莫对我厌恶，
莫谈我变色，
在社会主义的舞台，
我扮着壮丽的角色：
我是国民经济的杠杆，
我是财政收入的脉搏，
我是国家大厦的基石，
我是绵绣山河的织梭。

我来自人民的乳汁，
又献身于母亲的魂魄。
变成了——

边防的铜墙铁壁，
工厂的汽笛高歌，
村寨的稻菽飘香，
科研的鲜花朵朵。
换来了——
市场货物琳琅满目，
学府殿堂龙藏虎卧，
柳下情人蜜语窃窃，
庭院爷孙嘻笑咯咯。

我也有我的尊严，
我也有我的性格：
依法缴纳——不避亲友，
按率计征——锱铢必索。
为了人民的幸福，
容不得偷漏骗拖；
为了国家的昌盛，
容不得权贵干涉。
谁要把我当作面团，
轻者我对他经济制裁，
重者自有刑罚的枷锁。

是的，

我伴随着国家的诞生而诞生，

我成长于历史的滚滚长河。

当然，

我也会随着国家的消亡而消失，

当我完成自身的社会职责。

那时，

也许会变成《资本论》续篇的字母，

也许会变成《史记》新编的文墨，

也许会成为课堂上的生词，

也许会成为太空里的尘末……

呵，这就是税，

呵，这就是我，

不，这是 TAX 的自白，

一支税的歌。

TAX Confessions

I am the TAX,
TAX is me,
I am the law,
I am jade and silk,
I am a contributor...
No, I am who I am.

Do not dislike me,
Do not turn pale when talking about me,
On the stage of socialism,
I am playing a magnificent role:
I am the lever of national economy,
I am the pulse of fiscal revenue,
I am the cornerstone of the nation,
I am a weaving shuttle that embroiders mountains and rivers.

I come from the people's providing,
And devote myself to the people.
I have become—
The copper and iron walls of border defense,
The factory's singing whistle,
The fragrant rice in the village,
The blooming flowers of scientific research.
I get in exchange—
The market filled with a dazzling array of goods,

The collages hiding dragons and crouching tigers,
Lovers under the willows whispering to each other,
Grandfather and grandson in the courtyard laughing happily.

I also have my dignity,
I also have my own personality:
Pay in accordance with the law—regardless of whether they are relatives or friends,
Rate—based taxation—every penny must be demanded.
For the happiness of the people,
There is no room for leakage, deception, or procrastination;
For the prosperity of the country,
There is toleration of the interference from powerful officials.
Whoever wants to treat me like dough,
I will impose economic sanctions on him if the case is minor,
Or impose shackles of punishment if the case is severe.

Yes,
I was born with the birth of my country,
I grew up in the rolling river of history.
Of course,
I will also disappear with the demise of the country,

When I fulfill my social responsibilities.
At that time,
Perhaps it will become a letter in the sequel to *Capital,*
Perhaps it will become a new edition of story in the *Records of the Historian*,
Perhaps it will become a new word in the classroom,
Perhaps it will become dust in space...

Oh, this is the tax,
Oh, this is me,
No, this is TAX's confession,
This is a tax song.

小　河

喧嚣的农贸市场，
像一条欢腾的河。
货物、人流、声的波浪，
在唱着一支欢快的歌。

一头流来乡村的笑，
一头涌来城镇的乐。
流走了昔日层层的汗，
浮起了今朝生活的涡。

透过道道回荡的水，
我看到，春天的雨露秋季的果……
呵，这条欢腾的小河，
在唱着一支勤劳与生活的歌。

Small River

The bustling agricultural market
is like a joyful river.
The waves of goods, people, and sound
are singing a cheerful song.

A smile flows from the countryside in one end,
A burst of joy surges into the town in the other end.
Washing away is the layer of sweat from the past,
Floating up is the vortex of today's life.

Through the echoing water,
I see the rain and dew of spring, the fruits of autumn...
Oh, this joyful little river,
Is singing a song of diligence and life.

雷　声

山谷格外静，
蓝天分外明。
腐叶松如毯，
绿苔滑似绒。

举步攀险峰，
忽闻霹雳声。
吓得群山抖呵，
唬得地颤动……

抬头不见雨，
何来雷轰鸣?
身旁大伯微微笑:
“致富路，开山放炮声。”

Thunder

The valley is particularly quiet,
The blue sky is particularly bright.
Rotten pine leaves are like a carpet,
The green moss is as smooth as velvet.

Step up the dangerous peak,
Suddenly heard a thunderous sound.
Startled, the mountains trembled,
Trembling with fear...

Look up but not seeing the rain,
Why does the thunder roar?
An uncle beside me smiled slightly:
"Building road to wealth and the sound is blasting mountains for it."

夏至寄友

时值夏至，

夏已至盛、夜短昼长。

在这个万物竞生的季节里，

愿你满怀希望、展翅翱翔；

望你不负时光，

勇敢追逐自己的梦想。

相信你所有的汗水和愿望，

终会叶茂花香。

To Friends on Summer Solstice

At the summer solstice,

Summer has reached its peak, with short nights and long days.

In this season when all things are growing,

May you soar with hope and spread your wings;

I hope you live up to your time,

Courageously pursue your own dreams.

Believe in all your sweat and wishes,

Eventually, there will be lush leaves and fragrant flowers.

新民歌三首

收割

不用镰刀不打场，
不劳天风吹谷糠。
只要收割机地里跑，
庄稼乖乖进粮仓。

耕地

银犁闪闪无人奔，
泥浪滚涌连天门。
吃惊牛郎拨云望，
不知耕地是何神？

越唱胸中歌越多

农村新貌不胜说，
千言万语涌心窝。
金歌银曲唱不尽，
越唱胸中歌越多。

Three New Folk Songs

1. Harvest

No need for reaping with a sickle or threshing like a hundred years ago,
No need for the wind to blow the bran.
As long as the harvester runs in the field,
The crops obediently enter the granary.

2. Cultivate Land

The silver plow sparkles and no one besides them,
Mud waves roll and surge, connecting to Tianmen.
Surprised Cowherd looks down through the clouds,
Who is the god of farmland?

3. The more you sing, the more songs you have in your heart

The new appearance of rural areas is indescribable,
Thousands of words flood my heart.
Good songs cannot be fully sung,
The more you sing, the more songs you have in your heart.

我想当一个科学家（儿歌）

小喜鹊，叫喳喳，

我问喜鹊你叫啥?

喜鹊对我点点头，

叽叽喳喳说了话:

今天天气真是好，

东西南北我去耍。

叫声喜鹊别去啦，

没见叔叔阿姨搞“四化”?

咱们也要加把油，

不能天天贪玩耍。

你去地里多捉虫，

我到学校学文化。

你当庄稼的好哨兵，

我当一个好娃娃，

不，我当一个科学家!

I Want to Be a Scientist (Nursery Rhyme)

Little magpie, is chirping,
What are you saying , Magpie?
The magpie nods at me,
Chatting and talking:
The weather is really nice today,
I'll go play around everywhere.
Call magpies, do not go,
Haven't you seen Uncle and Auntie engaging
in the 'Four Modernizations'?
You also need to give a hard,
Instead of indulging in playing every day.
You catch more insects in the field,
I learn more knowledge at school.
You will be a good sentinel for the crops,
I will be a good child for my parents,
No, I will be a scientist!

春天里

春天里，
飘着若有若无的雾雨，
那是老人慈祥的笑意。

春天里，
落着绵绵的细雨，
那是知己无言的思绪。

春天里，
空气湿润润儿地，
似婴儿浴后透着自然的香气。

春天里，
下着迷蒙的小雨，
那是她的湿唇吻着我的脸和身体。

春天里，
我漫步在这春的大地，
陶醉在了这春的气息。

In Spring

In spring,
Floating with a misty rain that is elusive
is the kind smile of the old man.

In spring,
With a continuous drizzle falling,
Are the unspoken thoughts of close friends.

In spring,
The air is moist,
Smells like a natural baby bath.

In spring,
The hazy light rain drizzling,
Is her wet lips kissing my face and body.

In spring,
I stroll on this spring land,
Immersed in the scent of spring.

想之梦

秋意把路边的树木染成了金色，
落叶飘然地覆盖着大地。
在这个转瞬即逝的季节里，
我在梦中想起你。

你的音容笑貌，
你的深情厚谊，
你的一切的一切，
深深地刻在了我的记忆里。

溪水也许可以枯竭，
花草也会轮回四季。
但是我们相聚的时光，
却让我无法忘记。

也许是前世的缘分，
也许是今生的心意，
也许是来世的期许，
让我怎能不想你。

Dream of Thoughts

Autumn has dyed the roadside trees golden,
Fallen leaves cover the earth.
In this fleeting season,
I miss you in the dream.

Your appearance and smile,
Your profound friendship,
Everything about you, everything,
Have been deeply engraved in my memory.

The stream may dry up,
Flowers and plants also cycle through the four seasons.
But the time we spend together
Makes me unable to forget.

Perhaps it's fate from the past life,
Perhaps it is the intention of this life,
Perhaps it is an expectation for the afterlife,
How could I not miss you?

一碗鸡汤

下乡到山洼，
住在大娘家。
春风送暖鸟儿鸣，
山村颂佳话。

劈山修渠锁蛟龙，
引水筑大坝。
火热工地甩热汗，
不慎将脚砸。

抬下火线回到家，
忽闻鸡声哑。
吧嗒一声门帘响，
大娘站炕下。

一碗鸡汤手上端，
漂满香油花。
热气轻拂大娘面，
微笑把话答：

“孩子，快喝汤，
保养身骨架。”
手捧汤碗身心暖，
泪珠砸油花。

大娘银白鬓发上，
我似看到妈；
大娘额头皱纹里，
使我想到爸。

“又麻烦您老人家！”
“说的哪里话？”
大娘坐在炕边上，
闻言笑哈哈：

“俺村就是恁的家，
不能说外话！”
话语似洪钟，
震荡山洼洼。

不觉伤痛减三分，

精神成倍加。

春催山花遍野开，

映红天边霞。

A Bowl of Chicken Soup

Once I went to the countryside to the valley
Living in an auntie's home.
The spring breeze brought warmth and birds sang,
It was as a good story spread in the mountain village.

Cutting mountains, repairing canals, and halting flow of water,
Water diversion and dam construction.
Sweating profusely at a hot construction site,
I accidentally got my foot hit.

Lifted down the firing line I returned to the house,
Suddenly I heard the hoarse sound of a chicken.
With a click of the door curtain,
Auntie stood beside the bed.

A bowl of chicken soup was held in her hand,

Floating with fragrant oil.
The hot air gently brushed against the face of the old lady,
She smiled and answered:

"Child, have some soup quickly,
And be healthy."
Holding the bowl in my hand, I felt warm in the body and mind,
My tears smashed the oil droplets.

From Auntie's silver hair,
I seemed to see my mom;
The wrinkles on the forehead of the old lady,
Reminded me of my dad.

"Sorry to bother you again, Granny!"
"Do not say that."
Auntie sat by the bed,
Laughing when listening to the words:

"Our village is your home,
You can't talk like that!"
Loud voice was like a bell,
Shaking mountains and valleys.

Unconsciously my pain reduced a lot,
My spirit was doubled.
Spring made flowers bloom everywhere,
Reflecting the red sky and rosy clouds on the horizon.

落　叶

秋深了，
叶虽然留恋枝头的余香和繁茂，
也只能无奈地随着风吟诗舞蹈。

叶潇洒地扭着腰肢，
在空中自由自在地飘摇，
向大树投去了最后的一瞥。

虽然仅仅是一枚落叶，
但它也走过了春夏、经历过雨霜，
仍不失一个灵性生命的情操。

虽然会从这个世上化为泥土，
叶仍觉得秋成全了它的美丽，
它也顺遂了秋的心潮。

秋深了，
落叶蕴含了世间无限的韵味，
亦彰显了这个季节的美好。

Fallen Leaf

Autumn is deep,
Although the leaf lingers on the lingering fragrance and lush foliage of the branches,
It can only helplessly recite poetry and dance with the wind.

It twists its waist gracefully,
Swinging freely in the air,
It casts a final glance towards the big tree.

Although it is just a fallen leaf,
It has also gone through spring and summer, experienced rain and frost,
Still maintaining the sentiment of a spiritual life.

Although it will turn into soil in this world,
It still feels that autumn has fulfilled its beauty,
It also follows the tide of autumn's heart.

Autumn is deep,
Fallen leaves contain infinite charm in the world,
They also show the beauty of this season.

人　生

人生如河，

必有平静和风波；

人生如歌，

要忍耐高亢与曲折。

人生如戏，

不必在意大小角色；

人生如画，

不必在意轻描重墨。

人生如酒，

要品尝甘苦和香涩；

人生如火，

要释放能量温暖家国。

人生如烛，

光亮如豆奉献并不逊色；

人生如航，

平安就是最大的收获。

人生如梦，

如果装睡便倏忽已没；

人生如旅，

努力前行便不枉来过。

Life

Life is like a river,

There must be calmness and turmoil;

Life is like a song,

Should be patient with highs and lows.

Life is like a play,

Do not worry about whether the characters are big or small;

Life is like a painting,

Do not worry about light strokes and heavy ink.

Life is like wine,

Tasting sweet, bitter or astringent;

Life is like fire,

Releasing energy to warm our family and motherland.

Life is like a candle,
Radiant as beans, dedication is not inferior;
Life is like a voyage,
Peace is the greatest harvest.

Life is like a dream,
If you pretend to be asleep, it will suddenly disappear;
Life is like a journey,
Striving forward will not be in vain.

家乡的湖

家乡的湖就在家的门前，
像一块巨大的翠玉镶在家的旁边。
看着这个美丽的财富，
想想就觉得心里香甜。

它圆了黄河的一个梦想，
它解了龙乡的一个心愿。
扫除了沙丘的黄色风尘，
赶跑了地水的白色盐碱。

荷叶下鱼在游戏南北，
湖面上船在东西浏览；
湖心岛的芦苇招来了天鹅，
岸边的花草让人流连忘返。

湖边沙滩孩子们在尽情嬉戏，
树荫长廊老人们喝茶聊天，
跑道上青年人在自行赛车，
环湖音乐是那么的悠然。

湖是儿时难忘的回忆，
湖是今日的白云蓝天。
湖是华夏龙遥远的故乡，
湖是时光灿烂的诗篇。

那南北彩虹是湖的翅膀，
那蚌壳图腾是六千年的沉淀。
我的家在黄河故道上，
家乡的湖是老区的心田。

Lake in My Hometown

The lake in my hometown is right in front of my doorstep,
Like a huge emerald inlaid next to the house.
Looking at this beautiful wealth,
I feel sweet in my heart.

It fulfills a dream of the Yellow River,
It fulfills a wish of the hometown of Chinese dragon.
Sweep away the yellow dust from the sand dunes,
Drive away the white saline alkali in the ground water.

Fish under lotus leaves are playing from north to south,
The boat on the lake is navigating from east to west;
The reeds on the central island of the lake attract swans,
The flowers and plants on the shore are too beautiful that people forget to leave.

The children are playing and frolicking on the beach by the lake,
The old people are drinking tea and chatting in the long corridor under the shade of trees,
Young people are racing bicycles on the track,
The music around the lake is so leisurely.

The lake is an unforgettable childhood memory,
The lake is today's white clouds and blue sky.
The lake is the distant homeland of the Chinese dragon,
The lake is a brilliant poem of time.

The north—south rainbow is the wings of the lake,
That clamshell totem is a sediment of six thousand years.
My home is on the old course of the Yellow River,
The lake in my hometown is the heart of the old district.

龙湖的风

龙湖的风一阵阵吹来，
揉碎了湖中的冰凌；
在逐渐消失的冰盖下，
放出了春的萌动。

龙湖的风一阵阵拂过，
荷叶的腰肢快乐地扭动；
湖面像一匹巨大的绸缎，
褶皱被一次次拉伸抚平。

龙湖的风一阵阵刮过，
把一群群野鸭变成了精灵；
为小船擦去满头的汗水，
把两岸染成了金色苍穹。

龙湖的风一阵阵吹过，
赶走了雾霾还龙湖一个清静；
让雪花一朵朵融入湖水，
孕育和酝酿着新的生命。

龙湖的风轻轻地走来，
我看到了你的身影；
清澈的湖水是你的眼波，
靓丽的龙湖是你的面容。

The Wind of Longhu Lake

The wind of Longhu Lake blows in waves,
Shattering the ice in the lake;
The gradually disappearing ice sheet under it
is releasing the sprouting of spring.

The wind of Longhu Lake brushes past in waves,
The lotus leaf's waist twists happily;
The lake surface is like a huge silk,
The wrinkles are stretched and smoothed out time and time again.

The wind in Longhu Lake blows in waves,
Transforming flocks of wild ducks into elves;
Wiping away the sweat from the small boat,
And staining both sides of the strait into a golden sky.

The wind in Longhu Lake blows in waves,
Driving away haze and returning clear air to it;
Letting the snowflakes blend into the lake one by one,
Nurturing and brewing new life.

The wind of Longhu Lake comes gently,
I see your figure;
The clear water is your eye waves,
The beautiful lake is your face.

送 别

你就这样傻傻地走了，
留下我孤独的惆怅；
你就这样默默地走了，
抛弃了我们努力的事业和辉煌；
你就这样狠心地走了，
不顾我的留恋和感伤。

也许我们在一起的日子已久，
但我的感觉好像不长；
也许我们在一起时我没有好好珍惜，
你走后我发现失去了臂膀；
也许我们在一起时我对你有些严厉，
你走后我发现我是你的兄长。
望着你渐渐远去的身影，
我看到了大树的骨干、房屋的栋梁；
我真的怀疑我们多年共创的事业，
还能否、还能否再现昔日的阳光。

哎，你走吧、你走吧，

虽然我们曾经长相依，

如今只能逐渐相忘。

你走吧，你走吧，

可能把你留住是一种自私，

也许你能够展开理想的翅膀。

你，一定要走好啊，

在没有我陪伴的岁月里，

前边的路还遥远、漫长——

Farewell

You left foolishly like this,

Leaving me behind lonely and melancholy;

You left silently,

Abandoning our hard work and glory;

You left cruelly,

Disregarding my nostalgia and sadness.

Perhaps we have been together for a long time,

But it seems not so long for me;

Perhaps I did not cherish it when we were together,
After you left, I find that it seems like I had lost my arm;
Perhaps I was a bit strict with you when we were together,
After you left, I find out that I am your elder brother.
Watching your figure gradually fade away,
I see the backbone of a big tree and the pillars of a house;
I really doubt the career we have created together for many years,
Can we still recreate the sunshine of the past?

Hey, off you go, off you go,
Although we have previously been long together,
Now we can only gradually forget each other.
Off you go, off you go,
Perhaps keeping you here is selfish,
Perhaps you can spread your ideal wings.
You must take good care of yourself,
In the years without my company,
The road ahead is still far and long—

想　起

春天，岁月悠远，

好像我忘了你，

你也忘了我。

蓦然，看到了微信，

记起了我一个无效的生日，

哦，亲，祝你生日快乐！

I Remember

In spring, a long progression of years,

It seems as if I've forgotten you,

You also have forgotten me.

Suddenly, I look at WeChat,

Remembering my invalid birthday,

Oh, wish you a happy birthday!

我　说

一个尊贵的朋友问我，
幸福是什么？
我淡淡地微笑，
“幸福其实就是平安平静平常”，我说。

你若善待平常的生活，
人生就会变得五颜六色；
你若斤斤计较，前呼后拥也不开心，
你若纠结过往，锦衣玉食也难快乐。

幸福是内心的一种安然，
幸福是心灵感知的触摸；
幸福是生命的目标，
幸福也是境界的收获。

你可以说这是三言两拍，
你可以说这是红楼假说。
你也可以认为金玉良言，
你也可以认为消极超脱。

但是，

当你看到远方的饥饿与战火；

当你知道贪官锒铛入狱的下场，

当你感受病痛的威胁和折磨——

你会庆幸你国土的安乐，

你会珍惜你辛勤的劳作，

你会爱护你平淡的日子，

你会赞同我的述说。

I Say

A distinguished friend asked me
What was happiness?
I smiled faintly,
"Happiness is actually peace, tranquility, and normalcy," I said.

If you treat your ordinary life kindly,
Life will become colorful;

If you are too mean, you won't be happy even if being accompanied by a large retinue,
If you dwell on the past, you won't be happy even with luxurious clothing and food.

Happiness is a kind of inner peace,
Happiness is the touch perceived by the soul;
Happiness is the goal of life,
Happiness is also a harvest of realm.

You can say this is San Yan and Er Pai,
You can say that this is the Red Mansion hypothesis.
You can also consider them as valuable words as good advice,
You can also consider it as negative detachment.

However,
When you see hunger and war in the distance;
When you know the consequences of corrupt officials being imprisoned,
When you feel the threat and torment of illness——

You will be grateful for the peace and happiness of your homeland,
You will cherish your hard work,
You will cherish your ordinary days,
You will agree with my statement.

歌 者

我唱歌了，
悄悄地轻轻地哼哼；
抒发着心里的快意，
也许不会把人吵醒。

我唱歌了，
没有晦涩生冷，
没有异域照搬，
也没有粗鲁煽情。

我唱歌了，
有一丝唐宋遗风，
有一丝社会生活，
有一丝大众心声。

我唱歌了，
有诗歌应有的美景，
有诗歌简约的音韵，
也有中华歌谣的身影。

我唱歌了，
没有书袋层层，
没有标语口号，
也没有谁都不懂。

我唱歌了，
真的，唱的是自家的歌，
浅吟新诗的魅力，
深唱华夏文化的传承。

我唱歌了，
唱得悠悠轻轻；
唱着心中画意的春天，
唱着一个长长的美梦。

Singer

I sing,
Humming quietly and softly;
Expressing the joy in my heart,
Maybe it won't wake people up.

I sing,
There is no obscurity or hard—unelerstanding,
Without copying from other places,
There is no rude sentimentality either.

I sing,
That sounds a little bit like Tang and Song Dynasty legacy,
That contains a little bit of social life,
That contains a little bit of public sentiment.

I sing,
Which has beautiful scenery that poetry should have,
Which has a simple rhyme,
Which also has figures of Chinese folk songs.

I sing,
Without layers of book bags,
Without slogans,
Without hard understanding either.

I sing,
Really, I'm singing my own song,
Singing the charm of chanting new poetry,
Singing the inheritance of Chinese culture.

I sing,
Singing softly and leisurely;
Singing the picturesque spring in my heart,
Singing a long beautiful dream.

日 子

日子是什么，
是油盐酱醋茶白菜大葱?
是事业爱情票子孩子房子?
是也不是，它其实就是你的心情。

它有时就是时间，
变换着日旬月和春夏秋冬；
你可以自由散漫放手失去，
你可以奋力拼搏分秒必争。

它有时就是一桌饭，
酸甜苦辣咸淡凉热气腾腾；
你可以青菜萝卜一人品尝，
你可以鸡鸭鱼肉喝亲邀朋。

它有时是你望穿秋水的期待，
它有时是你不期而遇的圆梦，
它有时是你埋头拉车的汗水和熬煎，
它有时是你春风得意的鲜花和掌声。

有时它就像一杯白开水一样平淡，
有时它就像一壶老酒一样香浓。
有时它就是你的生命，
不珍惜，就不会健康安宁。

日子不能从过去重新开始，
它却可以从现在发生。
日子怎么过——幸福或者痛苦，
其实，它就在你自己的手中。

Days

What is a day?
Is it oil, salt, sauce, vinegar, tea, cabbage or scallions?
Is it a career, love, money, child or house?
Yes or no, it's actually determind your mood.

Sometimes it is just time,
With the day, ten days, month, spring, summer, autumn, and winter changing;

Which you can freely let go and lose,
In which you can work hard and seize every minute.

Sometimes it is just a meal,
Sweet, sour, bitter, spicy, salty, light, cool, and steaming hot;
You can taste vegetables and carrots alone,
You can also invite friends to taste chicken, duck, fish, and meat.

Sometimes it is your long—awaited expectation,
Sometimes it is just a dream that comes true unexpectedly,
Sometimes it is just the sweat and torture of burying your head in pulling the carts,
It can sometimes be your triumphant flowers and applause.

Sometimes it is as plain as a cup of plain water,
Sometimes it is as rich and fragrant as a pot of old wine.
Sometimes it is your life,
Without cherishing, you will not be healthy and peaceful.

Days cannot start over again from the past,
But it can happen from now on.
How to live life—happiness or pain,
Actually, it is in your own hands.

你来了吗

冬天，你来了吗?
草还在弱绿，树还在暗青;
虽然没有冰雪严寒，
依然刮着凛冽的北风。

望着夜空里的星星，
想起了你迷人的眼睛;
看到早晨的阳光，
记起了你淡淡的笑容。

虽然你脾气急躁，
朔风横扫尽显坦诚;
虽然你性格执拗，
雨雪纷飞滋润苍生。

你是四季的白色光环，
你是生命的循环时钟。
希望你如期而至呵，
因为我闻到了你身后醉人的春风。

Are You Here?

Are you here, winter?
The grass is still weak green, and the trees are still dark green;
Although it is not as cold as ice and snow,
There is still cold north wind blowing.

Looking at the stars in the night sky,
I remembered your enchanting eyes;
Seeing the morning sunshine,
I remembered your faint smile.

Although you have a hot temper,
The sweeping of the winter wind reveals honesty;
Although you have a stubborn personality,
Rain and snow flutter and nourish the world.

You are the white halo of the four seasons,
You are the cyclical clock of life.
I hope you come following the schedule,
Because I smelled the intoxicating spring breeze behind you.

有　你

此生此世因了有你，
才有了思念的远方，
才有了无尽的梦想，
才有了我心灵的故乡。

是喜是忧还是诗意?
是歌是画还是文章?
也许是情是谊或是迷茫，
也许是山是水亦是阳光。

你曾化为大雪中的一件毛衣，
你曾化为夏日里的一阵清凉，
你也曾化为久远的一声问候，
你也曾化为点赞的瞬间欢畅。

你从村头的泥塘中走来，
那是童言无忌的奔放。
你从小城深巷里走来，
那是两小无猜的回望。

你从高山流水里走来，
给予我灵魂安慰和荡漾；
你从广阔天地里走来，
给予我战胜困难的力量。

你从蓝天白云中走来，
有时是一碗烈酒的酣畅；
你从校园和军营中走来，
有时是悄然的红袖添香。

你从结义的桃园走来，
从此肝胆相照情谊刻在心上；
你从水泊梁山中走来，
从此不分贫富互助互帮……

呵，今生有你使我不枉此生，
今世有你世界更加明亮。
愿来世我们还能够相遇，
携手抑或是远方的凝望。

There You Are

It is only because of you in this life,
There is the distant place of longing,
There are endless dreams,
There is the homeland of my soul.

Is it joy, sorrow, or poetry?
Is it a song, a painting, or an article?
Perhaps it is friendship or confusion,
Perhaps it is mountains, water and sunshine.

You once turned into a sweater in the heavy snow,
You once transformed into a refreshing summer breeze,
You also turned into a distant greeting,
You also become the moments of joy when you give a thumbs—up.

You come from the mud pond at the end of the village,
That is the unrestrained expression of childhood.
You come from the deep alleys of the small town,
That is a look back from the two little ones.

You come from the high mountains and flowing water,
Giving my soul comfort and ripples;
You come from the vast world,

Giving me the strength to overcome difficulties.

You come from the blue sky and white clouds,
Sometimes you are the exhilaration of a bowl of strong liquor;
You come from the campus and military camp,
Sometimes you are a company of beauty.

You come from the peach orchard of brotherhood,
From then on, we treat each other in all sincerity;
You come from Mount Liang,
From that moment, we help each other no matter poor or rich...

Oh, knowing you in this life has made my life worthwhile,
With you in this world, the world is brighter.
Hope we can meet again in the afterlife,
Hand in hand or gazing from afar.

我多想

秋天散漫地脱去了一件件衣裳，
冬天裸露着肌肉来到了身旁。
我无奈地一步步离去，
无限的失落、无限的彷徨。

我多想留在你的身边，
做你坚强的脊梁；
为你仗剑撑起一把保护伞，
使你不再孤独、不再忧伤。

我多想和你在原野上纵情飞奔，
在蓝天下自由地吟唱，
在花丛中并肩漫步，
一起构筑春天的梦想。

我多想停下脚步，
和你在柳下窃窃私语、偷窥喜鹊，
在田埂听取蛙鸣、呼吸稻香，
一起陶醉夏天的时光。

梦想是那样的丰满，
现实是这样的骨感和惆怅。
这注定是命运的安排，
我们只能天各一方。

季节的心事绿黄转换，
岁月悠悠抚平一切的苍凉。
生活不能磨灭我的耐心和守望，
因为有诗、有剑，还有远方——

你是我心中的女神，
你是我永远的希望，
你是我生命的怀念，
呵，我的故乡！

I Really Want

In autumn, I casually take off my clothes one by one,
Winter comes to my side with bare muscles.
I leave step by step helplessly,
With infinite loss and infinite hesitation.

I really want to stay by your side,

Be your strong backbone;
Raise a protective umbrella for you with a sword,
Make you no longer lonely and sad.

I really want to run with you freely,
Singing freely under the blue sky,
Stroll side by side among the flowers,
Build the dream of spring together.

I really want to stop,
Whispering and peeping at magpies under the willows with you,
Listening to the chirping of frogs and breathing the fragrance of rice on the field ridge,
Indulging in the summer together.

Dreams are plump,
While reality is bony and melancholy.
This is definitely the arrangement of fate,
We can only go our separate ways.

Seasons' worries shift from green to yellow,
Time soothes all the desolation.
But life cannot erase my patience and watchfulness,
Because I have poetry, sword, and the distance—

You are the goddess in my heart,
You are my eternal hope,
You are the memory of my life,
Oh, my hometown!

致一位税务所长

饭店里你在端盘送碗，
大路旁你在补胎正圈，
田头上你为人殷勤理发，
党委会你在慷慨陈言……
好多人不知道你的名字，
人们亲切地喊你 “管得宽”。

盼相见，
常相见哟难相见！
凡有生活的地方，
就有你的足迹，
哪里有困难，
你就在哪里出现。

你为沙丘果林播下了芳香，
社队工厂的机鸣是你拨动的琴弦。
抗旱机井是你的汗珠汇成，
笔笔税款哟，是人民对你的礼赞！
对人民，

你是一汪流不尽的春水，

对投机分子，

你是一座威严的大山！

我爱你，

鲜明的憎爱，

火红的肝胆，

勤劳的标尺，

公正的戥盘。

所长同志哟，

你是真正的人民勤务员！

To a Tax Director

In the restaurant, you are serving dishes and bowls,

You are repairing the tire on the main road,

On the field, you diligently help and cut others' hair,

You are generously expressing your opinions in the Party Committee...

Many people do not know your name,

They affectionately call you "Busybody".

Looking forward to see each other,
We often hope to seeing each other, but it is hard to realize!
Wherever there is a place to live,
There are your footprints,
Wherever the difficulties are,
You are there.

You have sown fragrance for the sand dune fruit forest,
The sound of the machinery in the community factory is the strings you pluck.
Drought resistant wells are the result of your sweat,
The tax is a tribute to you from the people!
To the people,
You are an endless stream of spring water,
For speculators,
You are a majestic mountain!

I love you!
Distinctive abhorrence and love,
Heroic spirit and courage,
A diligent ruler,
A fair balance.

Comrade Director,
You are a true servant of the people!

新会计

新建队的新会计，
坐在窗前把账理，
手指上下似蝶舞，
算盘“啪啪”谱新曲。

咱队的新会计，
毛主席教导牢牢记，
“要节约闹革命”，
一分钱他掰成两五厘。

阴沟里吹来阵阵风，
乌云洒下点点雨：
“新建单位有后援，
多花一点没关系……”

咱们的新会计，
义正词严拍案起：
“‘有后援’也不该浪费，
何来的‘没关系’！”

“‘勤俭建国’是方针，
‘艰苦奋斗’是真理，
铺张浪费是犯罪，
多花半分我不依！”

句句如雷响，
声声震天际，
顶歪风，破迷雾，
有咱贫农的硬骨气！

新建队的新会计，
坐在窗前把账理，
算盘声声表心愿：
坚持乡村志不移！

原载《广阔天地新一代》诗歌集

New Accountant

The new accountant of the new team
Is sitting by the window, sorting out the accounts,
Fingers dance up and down like butterflies,
The abacus claps as if composing new songs.

Our team's new accountant
Remember Chairman Mao's words firmly,
"Be frugal to make revolution",
He uses a penny after thinking seriously.

Wind blows from the sewer,
Dark clouds cast a little rain:
"The newly established unit has backups,
It is okay to spend a little more... "

Our new accountant
Smites the table, rises up and says in stern and just words:
We should not waste even if we have backups,
Where does 'the okay' come from?

Building a country through thrift and hard work is the policy,
Hard work and struggle are the truth,
Extravagance and waste are crimes,

He even would not agree with spending a penny more.

Every sentence sounds like thunder,
The sound shakes the sky,
Against the bad tendencies, breaking through the mist,
He has the backbone of us poor farmers!

The new accountant of the new team
Is sitting by the window, sorting out the accounts,
Abacus voice expresses his wishes:
Build the rural spirit without moving!

辑三

Section Ⅲ

评　论

Comment

Section Ⅲ

“要留清白在人间”

——读《咏石灰》

千锤万凿出深山，
烈火焚烧若等闲；
粉骨碎身浑不怕，
要留清白在人间！[1]

这首气冲霄汉、铿锵动人的小诗，就是明朝军事家、政治家和诗人于谦的名诗《咏石灰》。五百多年来，它曾烧灼无数赤子的心，鼓舞人们坚持正义、不畏强暴，鼓励人们忠于职守、以身报国，因而为大家交口称赞，广泛流传。今天我们读来，仍有一定的教育意义和鼓舞作用。

作者于谦（1398—1457），字廷益，浙江省钱塘县人，明朝景帝年间任兵部尚书。据《明史》记载：“其才略开敏，精神周至，一时无与比。至性过人，忧国忘身。”[2]《咏石灰》大约是于谦十七岁（1414）时的作品。作者通过对石灰的赞咏，抒写了为正义事业不畏艰难、不怕牺牲、甘愿贡献的坚强意志，表现了诗人与污浊邪恶势不两立、保持终身清白的崇高情操。诗的前两句，描写了从开采矿石到烧成石灰的过程；后两句是说石灰粉碎后用来粉刷墙壁，它也是诗的高峰。诗人巧妙地借用石灰的粉碎和颜色，表达了自己的决心和意愿。《咏石灰》构思新奇，因而读来较前人“人生自古谁无死，留取丹心照汗青”，“生当作人杰，死亦为鬼雄”等传世佳句，更觉清新、生动。《咏石灰》不但情真意切，浑朴自然，明白易懂，而且音韵铿锵、富于感染力，我们不能不说是由于诗人驾驭语言的能力和在诗中注入了激越的情感、赤子的诚心所致。因而全诗读来，有咏之如江涛入怀、闻之若春雷横空、观之似高山瀑布之感，特别是“粉骨碎身浑不怕，要留清白在人间！”这样惊天地泣鬼神的佳句，尤使人性情陶冶、灵魂净化、受益匪浅。

诗如其人。《咏石灰》既是一首咏物言志抒情的千古绝句，又是诗人的誓言与终生的写照。明朝的统治发展到英宗时期，已开始走下坡路。当时，内有宦官王振等人专权，外有瓦剌部族虎视眈眈。然英宗朱祁镇却只知享福作乐，不问政事，终于导致了一四四九年秋的“土木之变”。英宗被俘，明朝五十万大军覆没，瓦剌首领也先率军兵临北京城下，明王朝危在旦夕。在这种情况下，坚守北京的兵部左侍郎于谦挺身而出，力主抗战，并亲自率领京城军民奋起迎击，激战五日，终于打退了瓦剌侵略军。北京保卫战的胜利，不但显示于谦在政治上的远见和军事上的才能，更充分表明了他“粉骨碎身浑不怕〞“烈火焚烧若等闲”的英雄气概和献身精神。此后，于谦辅助景帝朱祁钰安邦治国，日夜操劳，毫不考虑个人的恩怨、得失和安危，“毅然以社稷安危为己任”，[3]景帝赐他豪华的住所，他婉言谢绝，依然“自奉俭约，所居仅蔽风雨”。[4]宦官党羽、英宗复辟的黑干将石亨想讨好于谦，上疏要提拔于谦的儿子于冕，于谦当即予以痛斥，并声言：“我不希图意外的利益，决不让孩子滥用我的功名！”这与他当年“两袖清风朝天去”[5]不谄奉权奸的行为相辉映，构成了他为官清正、不谋私利、不畏奸邪、一心为国的清白品格。由于他处处以国家利益为准则，坚持抗战保边疆的正义立场，加之始终清廉刚直，不与宦官、奸党同流合污，因而遭到了一班权奸贵戚的嫉妒和恼恨。英宗和爪牙们趁景帝病危夺取东华门重登帝位后，于1457年2月杀害了于谦，但诗人清白的声誉却长留人间，当时民间流传着“鹭鸶水上走，何处觅鱼嗛（于谦）”等歌谣，表明了人民对他的深切怀念。

在解放思想、大干四化的今天，我们吟读《咏石灰》，要汲取“粉骨碎身浑不怕，要留清白在人间”的精神。在政治上刚正不阿，为了国家和人民的利益敢于坚持真理，实事求是，同一切不正之风和错误观念作不懈的斗争；在经济上则应廉洁奉公、不谋私利，保持和发扬我党艰苦奋斗的光荣传统与作风。对于每一个革命者来说，都应当具有这两个“清白”，并借以构织自己清白的历史，这样才不羞于古人，不愧为今人，不负于来人。同时，那些享受特权而不知足，随风而倒保纱帽，整日盘算家庭和子女的同志，不是也应从诗中有所受益吗？

【附注】

[1] 见《古代诗歌选》，少年儿童出版社，1962，第12页。

[2] 见张廷玉等撰《明史》，中华书局，第4549页。

[3] 见张廷玉等撰《明史》，中华书局，第4545页。

[4] 见《于谦和北京》，北京出版社，1961，第17页。

[5] 见《于谦和北京》，北京出版社，1961，第80页。

本文所用时间、数字、事例、人物、话语等，凡未注明的，均见《中国史纲要》第三册、《明史》及《于谦和北京》。

（原载《安阳文艺》1979年第2期）

凝练、生动、自然

——谈诗歌《漳河水》的语言艺术

高尔基曾经说过：语言是“文学的第一要素”。诗歌的语言对于诗歌来说，也起着这样的作用，我们的诗歌创作一定要在语言艺术上下功夫。那么，作为语言精华的诗歌，其语言艺术应该怎样运用和提高呢？这方面，为人们熟知和喜爱的叙事诗——阮章竞的《漳河水》，以它生动、凝练和朴素自然的语言特色，为我们提供了诗歌语言艺术有益的借鉴。

诗歌的语言必须高度凝练，言简意深，就是说要以最少的文字表达最多的内容。诗歌语言的凝练，是要经过反复推敲、千锤百炼的，但绝不是要过分雕琢、生冷晦涩，也不是刻意简古，那些从生活中、群众中来的纯朴语言，恰当运用就会收到凝练的效果。诗歌《漳河水》，通过对太行山下、漳河岸边三个妇女经过土地改革等斗争、打破封建牢笼、取得彻底翻身解放的不同遭遇的描写，充分展现了它语言艺术的魅力。首先，《漳河水》创作中，注意抓取人民群众口头上活的语言，并使之运用得恰到好处，从而使作品精炼含蓄，又妙趣横生。如“荷荷想配个‘抓心丹'，苓苓想许个‘如意郎'，紫金英想嫁个‘好到头'，毛毛小女不知道愁”。这里展示了，三个主人公向往自由、幸福的心理，由于运用了当时当地人民群众中间流行的对爱人的昵称，道出了荷荷想配个知冷知热心连心的丈夫，苓苓想要个情投意合又漂亮的男人，紫金英则想找个白头偕老长恩爱的伴侣，使得诗歌凝练、新颖，且生活气息浓郁。相形之下，其他词语在这里都会逊色。经济、简洁的文字概括地反映出丰富多彩的生活，语言高度凝练，再加上巧妙的构思等，使得作品更加含蓄蕴藉。如“种谷要种稀溜稠，娶妻要娶个剪发头”吟来朗朗上口，品之回味无穷。“稀溜稠”是当地老百姓的口头语，就是不能太稠了，要均匀种植;“剪发头”是当时形容那些思想进步、干劲大、敢于冲破封建藩篱的新式妇女的。如果作品直陈其事，则容易一览无余，无法把读者引入当时当地那个场景了，也就失去了人们常说的“诗味”。现在作品以口语入诗，可谓别开生面，不但乡土气息浓郁，而且起到了凝练含蓄的效果。

《漳河水》运用了绘声绘色、生动活泼的语言，使所勾勒的人物、场景形象鲜明。“低声拉话高声笑，好说个心事又好羞”，一下子抓住了所有少女性格的共同特征。荷荷、苓苓、紫金英虽然最后都得到了彻底翻身解放，然而她们走的道路不同，性格各自有异，诗歌运用生动、准确的语言，描绘了她们不同的性格特点。荷荷是个“只要咱行正脚立稳，谁要屈咱咱不答应”的女子，对于封建制度敢骂、敢冲，人们偷看她与王三好谈恋爱，她却说“戳破张麻纸五块钱，等我开门你进里面”，充分展现了她泼辣、大胆的性格。苓苓是个勤劳朴实的女子，在共产党员荷荷的带领下觉悟提高较快，三破丈夫老规矩，“一夜制服了个二老怪”。而紫金英则是个“话儿没完头低下，有语难明啃指甲”的性格软弱、温顺善良的女子，对于封建礼教的压迫，她只有对着墓生娃掉泪：“咽了吧，莫嫌苦，记住你娘是寡妇！”但是经过痛苦的斗争，最后也走上了新的道路。另外，如性格倔强、直爽的二老怪，顽守旧规、倒牙费嘴攻击新事物的张老嫂等，都在诗歌生动形象的语言勾勒下，跃然纸上。这些逼真感人的鲜明形象，是在篇幅有限、语句精炼的诗歌里纵横驰骋的，而诗歌并没有作正面的描写，只是通过生动的谈话、心理活动，显示出各自的特色来，这是我们叙事诗作者应当认真研究和借鉴的。另外，《漳河水》为了增强感情色彩和诗歌的艺术效果，还运用反复、比喻、夸张、拟人等修辞手法，使作品的语言更加生动、形象、活泼。作品也注意认真向民间歌谣学习，特别是开篇的《漳河小曲》和结尾的《牧羊小曲》，更是使人如闻其声、如临其境、如睹其色，可以说是首尾照应，生动始终。

《漳河水》语言的另一个特色，就是朴素自然、丰富多彩。我们有的诗歌语汇贫乏，反过来掉过去总是那么个“啊、呵、哟”和几个形容词，结果使得诗歌干瘪平淡、枯燥无味；也有的诗歌作者喜欢堆砌华丽的辞藻、玩弄文字游戏，甚至生造词语，他们不懂得什么叫朴素自然之美，仿佛只有辞藻华丽、语句艰涩才是好诗，殊不知这正是造成诗歌烦冗拖沓、以辞害意、妨碍思想内容的正确表达，致使诗歌僵化的重要原因。与之相反，《漳河水》认真学习人民群众的语言，从中选择和提炼那些有生命力的词汇，特别是把一些民谣、格言、歇后语和常用语等入诗，使得作品朴素、自然、亲切、真挚，而无雕琢刻板的痕迹，充满了生活的气息。描写苓苓的男人二老怪要打她时的心理："麻秆打她当挠痒痒，镐头一敲会死他娘！敲死人命可吃官司，不是坐牢就挨枪子！"写他大男子主义的碰壁是："母猪攻进棘针窝，自找苦吃自找祸。"作品在揭露和抨击封建制度对妇女的压迫与歧视时，批判了如"母猪不敬神，女人不算人""养孩儿抱蛋，洗衣裳做饭"以及"娶来的媳妇买来的马，任我骑来任我打"，那些"老王法""旧规矩"，不但加强了对封建礼教的鞭挞，歌颂了妇女解放的主题思想，而且也使诗歌通俗明畅、朴实自然、富于生活气息。诸如这类朴素自然的语言，在《漳河水》中俯拾皆是、不胜枚举，这也许是它为人们喜闻乐见的原因之一吧。

"语言这东西，不是随便可以学好的，非下苦功不可。"因此，我们的诗歌作者，一定要深入生活，认真地向人民群众学习语言，从生活中搜寻语言宝藏，淬炼好新诗的语言。同时还要从外国诗歌语言和我们古人诗词的语言中，吸取和借鉴有生命力的东西，使我们的诗歌语言生动、凝练、朴素，创作出无愧于我们时代的新诗来。

2023 年 7 月 13 日

浅谈民歌

民歌者，劳动人民的歌也。它贵就贵在一个“民”字上，内容必须是劳动人民的思想感情的反映，形式应当是特定的，为人民群众公认的短句式，语言则应是劳动人民的口头语。总之，从思想内容到表现形式都应该是劳动人民自己的东西。这就是民歌别于其它歌或诗的特色，也可以说是民歌味。否则，只能写成向民歌学习的新诗。

大跃进时期，湖北有首民歌：“我是喜鹊天上飞，社是山中一支梅，喜鹊落在梅树上，石滚打来也不飞。”读来脍炙人口。“喜鹊”“梅”“石滚”都是老百姓见惯了的东西，通过朴实的比兴，描绘出了人民群众一旦走上集体化的道路，就至死不回头的决心，歌颂了党在那个时期的中心任务。这首民歌之所以好，就在于它充分流露了人民群众自身的气质、风貌、精神状态。但是，目前我们有些同志对民歌认识不足，觉得只要七言四行（或五行）排列、明白如话，表达了政治内容就是好民歌。所以造成民歌创作上的下乘。有人把“劳动味”作为鉴别民歌真假及质量高低的“尺度”，准确与否有待讨论，不过它倒是指出了民歌思想内容方面的一个基本点，说明了民歌的特色。

民歌本是民心声，学诗更需学工农。要写出好的民歌，唱出人民群众的心声，就必须深入生活、深入群众，熟悉劳动者的语言，熟练地运用这些生动、朴实、活泼、洗炼的语言。如果不注意群众语言的运用，也会出现用自己的语言代替群众的语言、而使民歌逊色的毛病。有首民歌里有这样两句："铁手抡起钢镢头，叩着高山连声吼。"显然这里的"叩"字不是劳动者的语言，而是知识分子的口气，如果改成"敲"或"擂"，可能更符合群众的口气，从效果上也将更符合民歌豪放的格调。所以，我们的歌手要成为人民的代言人，要为人民而歌唱，就必须向工农群众学习，克服杂糅语言，掌握劳动者的语言，让我们的民歌手都放开金喉咙吧，让民歌插翅翱翔在中华民族的每一寸土地上吧！

（原载《安阳文艺》1978 年创刊号）

新诗要向民歌学习

新诗应向何处去？诗词大家、伟人毛泽东早就给我们指出了要向民歌学习的问题。新诗向民歌学习，不但代表了诗歌发展的趋向，而且也是我们更好地利用新诗进行艺术表达的需要；同时，也指明了民歌的地位。我们应当坚持新诗向民歌学习的正确方向。

新诗要向民歌学习，首先就必须对民歌有个正确的认识。民歌是劳动人民智慧的结晶，它代表了人民的思想和要求，反映了时代的精神与风貌。但是，对于这些朴素美丽的花朵，许多文人历来是看不起的，总是把它们看作是不登大雅之堂的“俚俗之辞”。因此，使得民歌艺术之花不能更好地展示姿容、放射芳香。而马克思主义文艺观历来就十分重视民歌。恩格斯曾热烈地称赞丹麦的一首反对封建贵族的民歌为最生动的歌，并亲自把它译成德文。毛泽东对民歌更是极为重视、大力支持，并且提出了新诗向民歌学习的问题。早在20世纪20年代，毛泽东在创办广东农民运动讲习所时，就曾亲自倡导搜集民歌。后来，毛泽东又提出要向民歌学习。同时也尖锐地指出：有些人不爱工农兵的“感情”和“姿态”，不爱他们的萌芽状态的文艺（墙报、壁画、民歌、民间故事等），批判了不重视民歌及其他民间艺术的错误倾向。到了20世纪50年代，毛泽东进一步指出要在学习民歌和古典诗歌的基础上，发展新诗创作。毛泽东对待民歌的态度和对新诗的要求，充分体现了马克思主义的文艺思想，给诗歌创作指出了一条光明大道。但是，长期以来一些人却对民歌这一光辉灿烂的艺术佳花大肆摧残，对新诗创作向民歌学习横加阻拦，一提及民歌，不是说“大多数是哥哥妹妹”，就是说是什么“打油诗”等。

新诗要向民歌学习，也是社会善于表达的需要。新诗应是各个时代的产物，中国的新诗应成为中国人民喜闻乐见的艺术形式。过去，在许多地方充斥着的是长而又长、散而又散的诗歌。有的靠堆砌华丽的辞藻，以显气势博大，诗章清奇；有的靠累叙复杂的过程，以便逐步“突出”其“英雄人物”；也有的盲目模仿外国诗歌的写作方式，违反汉语规则，没有韵味，词句朦胧隐晦，让人摸不着头脑……，凡此种种，不一而足。结果搞得面目全非，内容贫乏，语言晦涩，抹杀了诗歌的特色，冲淡了诗歌的诗味。因而，影响了诗歌的大众化，削弱了诗歌的艺术性。鲁迅先生说：“新诗先要有节调，押大致相近的韵”“记不住，就不能在人们的脑子里将旧诗挤出，占了它的地位。”这就告诉我们，新诗要精炼、大体整齐、押韵。诗贵精，贵在极少的文字，表达极大的激情和丰富的内容，使之活在人们的口上，刻在人们的心中。而民歌，在这方面正展示了它的英姿。在那“长夜难明赤县天”的时代，像“口唱山歌手插秧，汗珠滴尽谷满仓。牛出力来牛吃草，东家吃米我吃糠”这样如怨如诉的民歌，深刻地揭露了当时社会的黑暗，控诉和批判了那吃人的制度，广泛地流传在贫苦农民中间。在那“天连五岭银锄落”的建设年代，如“天上没有玉皇，地上没有龙王。我就是玉皇！我就是龙王！喝令三山五岳开道，我来了！”这样气吞山河的民歌，成了当时大家经常吟咏、鼓舞建设社会主义的精神力量。这些民歌之所以能够产生这样大的作用，主要是内容充实，反映了生活的本质，抒发了人民的强烈感情，然而，民歌本身的质朴自然，凝练易咏，活泼生动，不能不说是一个重要因素。新诗向民歌学习，就是要学习民歌强烈的大众性和思想性，学习民歌具有的一系列在艺术表现方面的优点，使新诗插上翅膀，更广泛地活跃在人民中间，发挥诗特有的作用。

新诗向民歌学习，也是诗歌发展本身所决定的。中国诗歌在其长期的发展中，在反复的讨论和实践中，也深感必须向民歌和古典诗歌学习。特别是民歌，更具有十分重要的意义。所谓“牧歌农谣诗本源”，虽不十分恰当，但也说明了一些问题。且不说民歌对《诗经》《离骚》等作品所起的巨大影响，也不讲李白、白居易等诗人如何汲取了民歌的营养，写出了许多不朽的诗篇，就拿“五四”以来新诗的情况来看，也可窥其一斑。“五四”时期，许多富有革命精神的优秀新诗出现了，但是有一些由于受西洋翻译诗的影响，离开我国的诗歌传统太远，所以不能在广大工农中间流传，在一定程度上减少了新诗的作用。毛主席《在延安文艺座谈会上的讲话》发表后，许多诗歌作者深入生活，向民歌学习，创作了许多深受人民大众欢迎的诗篇，如《王贵与李香香》等，就是这样的好作品。解放后，又出现了《回延安》等向民歌学习的好诗。特别是社会主义建设时期，大量优秀的民歌源源不断地涌现出来，这些新的民歌不仅是新时代的人民的诗歌，而且也有力地推动了新诗创作的发展。其中有些诗歌，至今仍为大家所吟咏和乐道。诗歌的发展说明，新诗向民歌学习非常有利于促进新诗具有“中国作风，中国气派”，更具有民族风格。“青山遮不住，毕竟东流去。”新诗向民歌学习的趋势，是不以人的意志为转移的。当然，新诗向民歌学习，应当是在其基础上前进。我们不否认有些民歌在长期的流传中，沾染了一些不良的东西，但是并不能因此抹去民歌的灿烂的光辉。我们也不否认，民歌艺术也还存在提高和发展的问题；同时，新民歌作为新诗的一种，怎样前进，也需要进一步商榷。这些也告诉我们，新诗向民歌学习绝不是简单照搬，也不是要新诗都写成一律的民歌体，而是要有选择地学习优秀的民歌，取彼之长，补新诗之短，并在此基础上有所创造、有所提高，坚持“百花齐放”推动诗歌的发展。这里我们还必须指出，新诗向民歌学习的过程中，应当遵照关于“古为今用，洋为中用”的方针，把向民歌学习与向古典诗歌学习、向外国优秀诗歌学习有机地结合起来。只有这样，才能使我们的新诗更加丰满、更加完善。

“请君莫奏前朝曲，听唱新翻杨柳枝”。今天社会主义的诗坛百花盛开，万紫千红。高歌吧，在向民歌学习的过程中，为开一代新的诗风而努力！

（原载《河南日报》1997 年 11 月 13 日第 3 版，有删减）

新诗要在传承中发展

诗歌作为文化艺术的一颗明珠，在人们精神世界和社会生活中不可忽视。美国诗论家梅·斯温逊在《科学时代诗的经验》中认为，“世界本质上是诗”。而我国古人早在春秋战国时期就指出“不学诗，无以言”。认为不学习诗，就无法发挥语言的表达能力。诗歌的地位是无可置疑的，但是在全球一体化和商业大潮的冲击下，其昔日风韵和光环已不再。如何创新和发展中国新诗歌，使之重新灿烂夺目，是值得我们认真探讨的。笔者认为，除了其他的途径，特别是要在汲取和传承中国优秀古典诗歌文化的基础上，创作出具有思想性、具有民族特色、群众喜爱的新诗歌。

一

新诗要在传承中发展，就要借鉴中华优秀古典诗词对思想情感的表达和社会功能的发挥。中国作为文化大国，诗歌历史悠久、艺术辉煌，是古往今来人们不可缺少的精神食粮。诗人用诗歌来表达自己的思想认知，诗歌作为一种文化也在影响着社会。

"诗者，志之所之也，在心为志，发言为诗。”古人认为，诗歌是用来表达思想、抒发感情的，人的思想感情存在于内心就是情志，用语言表达出来就是诗歌。诗歌是人们表达志向和愿望、追求个人目标和理想的一种方式。战国时期，中国浪漫主义诗歌的奠基人屈原，在长篇抒情诗《离骚》中倾诉了诗人对国家危亡的殷切关心，同时也体现了对百姓悲惨生活的关怀。“长太息以掩涕兮，哀民生之多艰。”面对战火四起，百姓生活艰难，屡被压榨，屈原的内心是熬煎的。为了寻找救国救民的道路，诗人“亦余心之所善兮，虽九死其犹未悔”，表明为了追求理想，虽九死也不动摇、不后悔的决心，体现出内心善洁、向往美好、追求崇高的境界。为保家卫国，唐朝诗人王昌龄则以“黄沙百战穿金甲，不破楼兰终不还”的诗句抒发了自己的情怀。唐末的农民起义领袖黄巢，在著名的咏物诗《题菊花》中，就以“他年我若为青帝，报与桃花一起开”的诗句，表达了打破不公、改变命运、翻身做主的雄心壮志。如果诗歌没有思想性，只有漂亮的语言和文字的技巧，是不会成为好诗的。新诗学习和借鉴古典诗歌，从思想和精神层面上来说，就是要继承古代诗人“不破楼兰终不还”的爱国情怀，“哀民生之多艰”的民本思想，以及旷达、进取的人生态度等，并在新时代发扬光大。

同时，诗歌不仅仅表现诗人一个人的内心情感，诗歌也是描述天下事的。优秀的古典诗歌往往强调作诗不仅在于述一己之穷通，更在于天下之哀乐。诗人应当通过诗歌的“兴观群怨”作用，颂扬真善美、贬斥假恶丑，从而发挥它“诗教”的社会功能。中国诗学从来看重诗对于世道人心的影响。中国有着悠久的诗教传统，诗教的说法最早见于《礼记·经解》篇。孔子说："其为人也，温柔敦厚，诗教也。"就是说君子的道德修养，是诗的修学培养的结果，是在学习之下的一种由内而外的体现。开中国古代诗歌先河的《诗经》，是中国第一部诗歌总集，西汉武帝以后被儒家尊为经典。它汇集了从西周初年到春秋中叶的305首诗歌，反映了这个时期的社会面貌。其中的《关雎》《伐檀》《硕鼠》等诗篇，更是传咏千古、为人乐道。鉴于《诗经》的成就，中国古代文艺理论认为"诗，可以兴，可以观，可以群，可以怨"，起到"诗教"的作用。中国古人认为，诗歌通过"兴"，用形象让人产生联想，激发情志，使之抒情言志，歌颂美好的事物。诗歌也可以通过对社会现象的观察和描写，观风俗之得失，因为它源于"饥者歌其食，劳者歌其事"，是有感而发的产物，因而必然是对它所诞生时代的真实反映。诗歌还可以加强与他人的交往，起到聚积友人、团结群众的作用。而最重要的是诗歌可以表达不满，表达对不公之事的怨诉，对社会政治进行讽谏，对不良现象作讽刺和批判。这一重要文化艺术观，被历代一直延续下来。

诗歌的教化和影响作用，是诗歌自身客观存在的。不管诗人是刻意书写，还是无意描绘，都会对亲人、朋友及周围人甚至世人，产生一定的影响。唐朝大诗人白居易的诗歌主张强调讽喻，补察时政，在《与元九书》中就直言："文章合为时而著，歌诗合为事而作。”目的就是要“唯歌生民病，愿得天子知”（《寄唐生》）。他的《卖炭翁》等许多诗歌都对统治者欺压和掠夺百姓进行了揭露，对当时社会的腐败给予了讽刺，因而有较大影响。北宋大词人苏东坡，因写了“岂是闻韶解忘味，迩来三月食无盐”和“东海若知明主意，应教斥卤变桑田”等诗篇，牵连进了“乌台诗案”，被指控谤讪宋神宗施行的盐禁政策和水利政策，结果被朝廷下狱、贬官，还连累了朋友和家人。而被誉为“千古词帝”的南唐后主李煜，却因一首凄美的《虞美人》词，于978年七夕生日时被宋太宗毒死。关于诗歌的教化和影响，“五四”新文化运动以后，郭沫若就提出：“诗的创造是要‘创造’人，换一句话便是在感情的美化。”其实，外国文艺理论对诗歌的教化作用，也有同样的认知。英国哲学家弗朗西斯·培根就认为“读诗使人灵秀”。而俄罗斯著名文艺理论家别林斯基更是认为，诗人“根据依存于对事物的看法，对生活内在的世界、时代和民族的态度的他固有的理想，来改造生活”。所以，我们说诗歌“诗教”的社会功能，是不能忽视的。

诗歌可以陶冶人的情操，它不仅是审美的，也是实用的。诗人透过诗歌不但表达自己的思想情感和志向，同时也通过自己个性化的表达和抒发，赋予了诗歌“兴、观、群、怨”的作用，借以发挥了诗歌教化的重要社会功能。这是我们的新诗在传承中华文化艺术、发展和创新诗歌中，应该借鉴和思考的。

二

新诗要在传承中发展，就要借鉴和汲取优秀古典诗词的创作艺术。诗歌作为文艺皇冠上的一颗明珠，它应当是美的，而这精美的文学形式，应当依照美的规律来塑造。所以，它对语言和艺术形式的要求是苛刻的，是需要对语言艺术进行较好地把握和运用的。这方面，优秀的中国古典诗词给我们提供了有益的借鉴。

中国古代诗论认为："诗言志，歌咏言。"诗是用来表达人的意志的，歌是咏唱诗的语言，以突出诗的意义。优秀的诗歌作品不仅应该表达出作者深刻的思想感情——"言志"，还需要具有优美的音乐性和节奏感——"咏言"。也就是说，诗歌作品应该既要注重其语言表达的情理含义，又要有优美的节律和音乐感，才能真正成为优秀的作品。这个观念在中国文学史上有着深远的影响，被认为是中国诗歌创作的重要原则之一。诗歌被称为文学之始、艺术之根。诗之为"诗"，就在于它是一种阐述心灵的文艺体裁，它需要一定的艺术技巧，并按照一定的音节和韵律的要求，用凝练的语言、丰富的情感和意境，高度集中地表现社会生活和人类精神世界。这就要求我们的新诗在表达个人情感和思想时，为突出诗歌的意义，必须运用好诗歌的语言。

其一，诗歌的语言要有一定的韵脚和节奏。由于诗歌属于韵文，在其最初的发展阶段，一般依据语音的自然节奏和口语的韵律而形成某种音乐性的效果。古人云：“无韵不成诗。”押韵为写诗填词的基本要求，是诗歌的一个主要特征。诗歌要有韵律和节奏，读来朗朗上口，便于记忆和传播，这也是其区别于小说、散文和其他文学艺术形式的特点。所以初学写诗者就要学习押韵。押韵作为诗的基本形式，能够增强读者朗诵和传咏的体验，便利诗歌的吟咏和流传。古典诗词中的词本是可以直接歌唱的。诗从其诞生伊始，便与音乐水乳交融。当然，新诗的押韵并非押格律诗的韵，新诗可以没有平仄，但不能没有韵脚，不能没有韵律感，要按照中国汉语拼音的韵母，押大致相同的韵脚就可以了。正如鲁迅先生所说：“诗须有形式，要易记，易懂，易唱，动听，但格式不要太严。要有韵，但不必依旧诗韵，只要顺口就好。”除了韵脚，诗歌的节律也是必不可少的。所谓节律就是诗的节奏和规律。一首诗歌是由一些诗节组成的，诗节是由符合汉语特点的诗行构成，而诗行是由音组与音组的组合而成。一般情况下五言绝句的节奏是“221”或者“212”，七言绝句一般为“223”等。比如孟浩然《春晓》的节奏为：“春眠/不觉/晓，处处/闻/啼鸟。夜来/风雨/声，花落/知/多少。”当然，新诗不必拘泥古典诗词的节律，可以根据诗行的长短，设定自己的节奏。一首诗歌，一般最好设定相近的节律，以使诗歌上下通畅、便于吟咏。

有些诗友认为中国诗歌需要与国际接轨，需要学习西方诗歌的创作方式，可以没有韵脚和节奏，这其实是一种误解。因为外国的诗歌同样也是有自己的语言文化特性和韵律的。意大利诗人但丁的长诗《神曲》，被誉为中世纪文学的巅峰，是采用三行诗节押韵法写成的。英国著名诗人雪莱于1819年写的《西风颂》，是其“三大颂”诗歌中的一首，是用五个十四行诗组成，以五音步抑扬格为主，其韵脚为ababcbcdcdedee，每个诗节在语法结构上彼此相连，浑然一体。而德国著名诗人歌德，往往使用双行体押韵诗和六音步诗来写作并赠人。特别是美国优美的小诗《雪绒花》，诗行有长有短，三、四行押韵，二、五行押韵，六、七行押韵，八、十行押韵，一、九行押韵，读起来朗朗上口，唱起来优美动听，深受各国人民的喜爱。之所以认为外国诗歌不押韵和节奏不畅，主要是对外国诗歌不了解或者是误解。作诗要有韵脚和节律，就像“戴着镣铐跳舞”。在这一点上，国内外的学术观点皆然，德国的诗人歌德和中国新诗著名诗人闻一多的观点也是一致的。诗歌的创作可以说是限制中有自由，自由中又有限制，是限制中的自由。新诗创作应该像是戴着镣铐跳舞，镣铐就是韵脚和节律。我们要大致上跟着韵脚和节律走，却又不完全受其拘束，要戴着镣铐跳出自己的新的舞步。

其二，诗歌的语言要凝练和含蓄。诗歌是字少意丰的文学艺术，诗歌的语言需要用凝练而含蓄的文字来表达。这就要求诗人在产生表达和抒发的欲望下，以简洁精美、凝练含蓄、音韵和谐、适于诵读的形式诉之于文字表达。优秀的古典诗词可用寥寥数语，甚至十几个字把世间景色、山河万物、人情世故等描述得绘形绘色。如李白的七言绝句《望天门山》只有四句，但是意境开阔、和谐流畅、语言凝练、色彩鲜明，描绘出一幅壮丽优美的画卷，表达出一种豪迈的气魄。唐朝诗人柳宗元的五言绝句《江雪》，则通过凝练、含蓄的语言勾画了独钓寒江的渔翁形象，借以表达了诗人在遭受打击之后不屈而又深感孤寂的情绪。这首短诗运用具体而细致的手法来摹写背景，运用远距离画面来描写主要形象，将精雕细琢和极度夸张糅合在一起，语言简洁凝练而意蕴丰富，全诗虽仅有20字，却描绘了一幅幽静寒冷的画面。特别是“寒江雪”三字作为点睛之笔，把诗前后两部分有机地联系起来，不但构成了一幅凝炼而概括的图景，也刻画了渔翁孤独而坚韧的形象。

诗歌是语言的艺术，诗歌创作的高级阶段是凝练、简约而不简单，看似用词不华丽而实则音韵意境俱有，看似简单而实则意味深长、回味无穷。所以优秀的古典诗词在创作上，着意于音律、对偶、字句的推敲锤炼，注重于炼字、炼句。虽描写琐细的日常生活情景，然清新优美的佳句比比皆是。唐代诗僧贾岛《题李凝幽居》诗的名句“鸟宿池边树，僧敲月下门”，初欲用“推”字，后改为“敲”字，两字哪个更好呢？他骑着驴边走边斟酌，直到撞了韩愈之后，韩愈建议用“敲”，这才定了下来。一个“敲”字，于幽静的环境、响中寓静，动静相衬，使意境更见幽迥。正是由于古代诗人为了获得凝练含蓄的佳句，而抱定“语不惊人死不休”的认真写作态度，本着“吟安一个字，捻断数茎须”的苦吟精神，因而有了“两句三年得，一吟双泪流”的艺术创造和效果，这才有了今天流传千古的金句和名篇。优秀古典诗词在创作过程中，这种反复吟咏、苦心推敲、严肃认真、一丝不苟的态度，正是现代诗歌作者所缺少和需要的。新诗在创作和发展中，要继承和发扬这种刻苦研讨、严谨创作的精神，使诗歌成为字字珠玑、句句金言的精彩篇章。这在生活节奏加快、人们越来越浮躁的今天，显得尤为重要。

其三，诗歌的语言描述要生动形象。诗歌要有诗的灵魂，即饱含深层意味的、感人心肺的“意境”，也就是所谓的“诗味”。它是诗的内涵和底蕴，也是能吸引读者去品味诗的艺术技能。因此，诗歌需要用优美的语言雕刻出隽永的形象和意境，需要让文字有音乐感和画面感，借以传递和展示思想情感。

中国是一个诗的国度，古典诗歌长期以来以不同的内容和形式，呈现着百花争妍、姹紫嫣红的状态。它们既有内容上的抒情诗和叙事诗，也有体裁形式上的古体诗和格律诗，既有题材上的田园诗，山水诗，边塞诗，闺中诗等，也有艺术表现上的现实主义和浪漫主义。这些诗歌或者婉约、或者豪迈、或者风雅、或者凄凉，既生动优美，又词语精炼，充满了诗情画意。中国古典诗歌之所以如此优美绚丽，除了其他因素，还在于创作中采取了“赋比兴”的艺术手法。所谓“赋”就是铺陈直叙的表现手法，“直书其事，寓言写物，赋也”（钟嵘《诗品序》）；“比”是比喻手法，即“以彼物比此物也”（朱熹《诗集传》）；“兴“”即起兴，指具有引发作用的手法，“先言他物以引起所咏之辞也”（朱熹《诗集传》）。古典诗词大都是说事然后及己，描绘的对象包罗万象，可以是高山大川，可以是江河湖海，可以是花鸟鱼虫，可以是林木稼穑，可以是天下万物，也可以是人间百态，运用“赋比兴”手法使得诗歌语言生动形象、意境优美且意义深刻。如屈原的《天问》诗中，运用大量的比喻等手法，体现了丰富的浪漫主义色彩。而在为数不多的古代叙事诗中，长达1700多字的叙事诗《孔雀东南飞》，除了发端两句用“孔雀东南飞，五里一徘徊”起“兴”外，通篇采用“赋”体，叙述出神入化。其后如北朝的《木兰诗》、杜甫的《石壕吏》，白居易的《卖炭翁》等，也都是运用“赋”法而表现出优异的特色。为了让诗歌意味无穷，生动感人，古典诗词理论还认为，真正的好诗，既不能单用“比兴”以致意深、晦涩，又不能单用“赋”法以致意浅、芜累，只有兼采三者之长，酌情运用，才能生动感人。诗歌要把事情描述清楚，让读者了解，就要用“赋”的手法，而诗歌要抒发情思、驰骋想象、感染读者并耐人寻味，就要用“比兴”的手法，通过这三种艺术手法的交替使用，把诗歌特殊的感人作用与艺术的思维表现特点联系起来，使诗歌产生应有的“滋味”。这些艺术手法的运用，是值得我们今天的新诗学习和借鉴的。常言说：诗是无形画，画是有形诗。这就要求诗歌不能使用散文和小说的语言，它应当短小精炼、抒情达意，而且是生动形象、具有色彩画面感。这样才能描绘出长河落日圆的优美或者八千里路云和月的豪迈，抒发出“安得广厦千万间，大庇天下寒士俱欢颜”的胸怀或者把栏杆拍遍的无奈，诉说出白发三千丈的忧愁或者怒斥健儿无粮百姓饥的病态，书写出壮美、凄美、恬美、韵律美的诗篇。

新诗要在传承中发展，就应当在艺术形式上具备和完善其基本的特质，既要抑扬顿挫有节奏感，也要合辙押韵有韵律感，既要炼字炼句精致优美，也要描境绘意含不尽之意于言外，使人思而得之。它不能像一杯白开水淡而无味，也不能不知所云晦涩难懂，否则就不能称其为好诗了。诗歌只有充分展现语言美、韵律美、节奏美、意境美、趣味美，才能够给人们带来美的享受。优秀的古典诗词语言优美、意境深远、形式多样，具有很强的艺术感染力和美学魅力，不仅可以让人在阅读中感受到心灵的愉悦和满足，还可以提高人们的文学鉴赏能力和审美素养。这也正是新诗创作中需要汲取的重要营养。

三

新诗要在传承中发展，就要具有本民族的文化艺术特色，借鉴优秀古典诗词紧贴生活和平民的大众性，让社会和人民群众喜爱并流传。诗歌的繁荣，需要有人读诗、学诗、论诗、写诗、留传诗，这就决定了诗歌的民族艺术性和大众性。如果将这颗艺术明珠仅作为少数人在圈子内的玩物，必然失去它应有的光彩。诗歌的形成和发展，离不开它的历史和环境。新诗如果脱离了它的源头，脱离了它赖以生存的脚下的土壤，脱离了现实生活，艺术之花就成了无源之水、无根之木，必然枯萎，其艺术也就不再成为艺术了。时代的进程是环环相扣的乐章，诗歌的发展是承上启下的和弦。中国新诗在传承和发展中，让它具有中华文化艺术的特色，成为人民群众喜闻乐见的艺术形式，是新诗的重要责任。

首先，新诗应当具有中国文化艺术特色，与外国诗歌艺术相互学习而不崇洋。

在国际化的潮流下，中国诗歌应该拥抱多元化，追求更全面的发展。那么是不是新诗应当模仿或者照搬西方的诗歌思维和形式呢？回答是否定的。鲁迅曾经指出：“（文化艺术）有地方色彩的，倒容易成为世界的，即为别国所注意。打出世界去，即于中国之活动有利。”这就告诉我们，包括诗歌在内的文学艺术，越是具有本民族特色的，越是容易被世界所接受和尊重，越是容易走上世界舞台，也就越有利于中国文化。这就从另一个侧面告诉我们，中国新诗的发展应该走自己的路子，走在传承中发展的道路上，单纯模仿和照搬别人的艺术，是没有生命力的。中华文化博大精深，中国诗歌经过千百年的传承和发展，形成了自己的形式和语法，有其独特的艺术特色和魅力。正是由于中国诗歌艺术经过千百年提炼升华，具有了自己的民族特征和艺术光彩，因而才被世界所认同并影响着世界。包括诗歌在内的中华文化，不但有自己的辉煌成果，而且始终和而不流，中而不倚，存异求同。这就要求我们的新诗，必须把握好诗歌发展中创新与守正之间的辩证关系。创新意味着更多国际化的探讨，学习和吸收国内外诗歌的精华，毫无疑问这是应该采取的措施，但是如果不注意坚守自己民族文化的根本，则可能带来一些错觉和迷失。守正则是要保持自己传统的优秀艺术基因，巩固已有的文化优势，发展好今天的诗歌艺术，为将来的诗歌道路打下坚实的基础。在新形势下，新诗应当平衡好这两者的关系，实现更为全面的发展。

对外来文化，我们始终秉持尊重差异、相互借鉴、融汇贯通的态度，既保持自身的文化特色，又不断吸纳世界文明的精华，从而使中华民族深厚的文化底蕴和强大的民族精神，得以延续和发扬。新诗的探索和百花齐放，不能抱着崇洋卑古的心态，以西式语法和创作方式为时尚，拿来当作创新并照此改造中国诗歌。各国有各国的语言，各民族有各民族的文化艺术特色，可以相互借鉴和学习，但是不宜照抄照搬。新诗的创新和发展，不仅仅建立在无数诗歌的基础上，更建立在各自民族文化的传承之上。要让作品扎根于本土，从生活中汲取艺术灵感，而不应脱离本土、脱离现实、脱离生活。正如著名文艺评论家别林斯基所说："诗人永远是自己民族精神的代表，以自己民族的眼睛观察事物并按下她的印记的。越是天才的诗人，他的作品越普遍，而越普遍的作品就越是民族的、独创的。”在全球化的今天，新诗需要在保持中国传统文化优势的基础上，发扬勤奋刻苦和不断创新的精神，吸收国际文坛优秀诗歌艺术，形成有中国特色的新诗歌。

新诗是古诗的传承与发展，它的确借鉴了西洋诗语言和形式自由的要素，但在创作中不能为了让新诗具有所谓的意象和无约束，而韵律不明、节奏混乱，随意断字断句。如果以不合中国语言构造为创新和时尚，以西语句法和词语为诗意，追求所谓象征主义，追求以奇特观念的联络和繁复的意象来解构诗的内涵，把一些个人化的东西让读者在迷茫困惑中嚼蜡，则谬矣！没有了汉字词语本身的韵律美、音乐美、凝练美、形式美，诗无以歌咏、无以朗诵，就背离了中国诗词的传统，也就没有了中国新诗的健康发展，自然不会被社会和民众所接受。可以说，新诗的发展也是一种文化的浸染和精神的熏陶，诗歌艺术不仅仅包括对创新的渴望，更包括对自己传统的尊重，要有对诗歌发展本身规律的敬畏。其实，在新文化运动早期闻一多的《死水》、郭沫若的《凤凰涅槃》、徐志摩的《再别康桥》等，以及新中国建设时期郭小川的《团泊洼的秋天》、李瑛的《生命是一片叶子》等优秀作品，都对新诗的创作做出了有益的探索。在这个多元化的世界里，我们只有在保持诗歌民族特色的同时，保持开放的心态，尊重和欣赏每一种文化的美，拥抱差异，学会共存，让新诗的发展在传承中创新，在借鉴中外优秀诗歌艺术的创新中发展，才能让我们的诗歌创作更加丰富多彩。

其次，新诗要具有大众性，要贴近生活、贴近群众、朴素自然、不泥古。

新诗要在传承中发展，是不是可以回到格律诗的轨道上去呢？回答仍然是否定的。从艺术层面上说，诗歌不是要回过头来去写格律体的旧诗，而是要守正创新、汲古吟今，着重领会古代诗人所创造的意境、神韵、禅悟、体物、赋形等诗学范畴，品尝雄浑、恬淡、优美、典雅、绮丽等风格特征，把握言意、形神、虚实、藏露等辩证关系，以及起兴、比拟、隐喻、反讽等各种表现手法，从而构建融汇古今、贯通中外、充满时代感与现代气息的诗学体系。格律诗过多的格式限制，使思维和语言的发挥受到阻碍，也阻碍了诗歌的创新和发展。所以新诗的发展应当坚持尊古而不复古，没有必要去完全遵循格律诗的旧框框。其实，只是近体诗在格律上要求严格，而古体诗则没有固定的、严格的格律要求。汉朝乐府民歌及以前的诗歌，都没有严格的格律。如东汉末年的《古诗十九首》，其语言不假雕琢，浅近自然，但又异常精炼，含义丰富，耐人寻味，在中国文学史上有着重要的地位。格律诗出现后，古代诗人们并不一味唯格律是从。如孟浩然的五律《舟中晓望》就不对仗。被后世诗论家誉为“唐人七言律诗第一”的《黄鹤楼》，连诗仙李白都叹服“眼前有景道不得，崔颢题诗在上头”，也是不协律的。南宋杨万里七言律诗《进退格寄张功父姜尧章》，就不一韵到底，而是押邻韵，即押大致相近的韵。所以我们今天的新诗，没有理由被一些过于严格的形式所束缚。鲁迅曾批评道："诗，歌，词，曲，我以为原是民间物，文人取为己有，越做越难懂，弄得变成僵石，他们就又去取一样，又来慢慢的绞死它。"现在新诗的发展，断不能再走这样的路子。大众性是中国特色社会主义文化建设的定位和基本属性之一。应当认识到，文化的大众化一旦达成大众文化，那么就有了永恒的生命。文化不走向人民大众，就不可能有新的发展。所以新诗不能走小众化的格律诗的老路，必须走具有大众性的新诗的新路，让新诗成为被大众所理解、为大众所传颂、为广大民众所欣赏和喜爱的艺术。

新诗要具有大众性，就要贴近现实社会、贴近现实生活。艺术源于生活，生活就是现实社会和人民大众的活动。新诗只有贴近社会现实，赋予其时代精神，才能反映真实的社会现状，才能具有感人喻世的艺术价值。中国古代体现了现实主义诗歌色彩的诗歌，如杜甫的"三吏""三别"，白居易的《琵琶行》《长恨歌》等，都是流传千古的诗篇。特别是白居易的诗，由于重写实、尚通俗，得到了各阶层人民的欢迎。当时自长安到江西，三四千里，凡乡校、佛寺、逆旅、行舟之中往往都有题写其诗者，士庶、僧徒、孀妇、处女之口，每每都有咏其诗者。当白居易去世时，数以万计的人前来参加其葬礼，洛阳城里的酒楼茶肆都停业三日以示哀悼。甚至唐宣宗李忱悲痛之极，亲自写下《吊白居易》挽诗一首，以示哀悼：

“童子解吟长恨曲，胡儿能唱琵琶篇。文章已满行人耳，一度思卿一怆然。”可见白居易的诗歌在当时已家喻户晓，深受社会和百姓喜爱，并享誉海内外。后人甚至认为，白居易的诗歌艺术远超李白和杜甫，似有一定道理。诗歌贴近生活、反映现实，就具有生命力。贴近生活就是要把生活文艺化，将文艺生活化，让新诗扎根其生长的泥土，要接地气，要和人民群众血脉相连，在传承民族已有诗歌艺术的基础上进行创新。就其内容来说，社会现实、生活现实都是诗歌的刻画对象。现实生活中，我们的时时刻刻都会成为快乐的诗、坚强的诗、浪漫的诗、激愤的诗……，甚至我们不经意间说的话，也会成为诗的词句。我们身边的万事万物都是诗歌的来源，只要我们留心观察，用心描写，记录生活，抒发情怀，我们的话语和生活的每一个细节，都会成为感人的诗歌。如此，新诗才能走出自我无病呻吟或故弄玄虚的小圈子，登上社会的大舞台。

诗歌要具有大众性，就必须贴近人民大众，被老百姓接受和喜欢。诗歌要贴近人民大众，就应当朴素自然、通俗易懂，展现其歌唱、吟咏、朗诵等艺术功能，让作品走入人民群众之中，成为老百姓喜闻乐见的艺术形式。就其形式来说，新诗应当具有鲜明的民族风格、民族形式和民族特色，要有中国诗歌自己的模样。毛泽东曾经指出：“将来趋势，很可能从民歌中吸引养料和形式，发展成为一套吸引广大读者的新体诗歌。”艺术产生于民间又流传于民间，它本身就是一种大众化的民间行为。在一个高素质、高文化程度的时代里，诗歌不应该越来越小众化，必须走向大众化。这并不影响它同样也会因时而变，成为社会的高雅艺术。可以说，大众化就是诗歌的起步处。在孔子的时代，《诗经》就已经是当时的流行歌曲与经典诗歌的大全了，其中《风》就是周代各地的民歌，也就是流行歌曲，它是通俗的，也是朴素自然的。大雅若俗，好的诗歌应该是用最日常的口语，写出优雅和丰满的诗意。南朝梁诗论家钟嵘，在我国第一部诗歌批评专著《诗品》中，就着力提倡“风”而反对玄言，主张音韵自然和谐而反对人为的声病说，主张“直寻”而反对用典，提出了一套比较系统的诗歌品评的标准。诗歌应当朴素自然，通俗易懂，辞藻只是一种修饰，并不是越华丽就越好。唐宋许多优秀的诗篇，语言简单却非常精炼，不事藻饰却能发挥诗的最大功能。看似没有什么艺术技巧，实则诗浑然天成，自然明了，可以洗涤人的心灵，陶冶情操，给人以美的享受。如李白的《独坐敬亭山》、骆宾王的《咏鹅》、北宋诗人邵雍的《山村咏怀》等诗篇皆如此。它们虽简简单单，却朗朗上口，妇孺可咏，农夫可知，得以流传千古。所以新诗要向朴素自然、通俗易懂、便于传咏、让人们喜闻乐见的方向发展，不但要贴近实际生活、贴近人民群众，还要向社会和人民群众学习鲜活的语言，并借鉴其大众化的艺术形式。

中国新诗的创作，应该在传承中华民族优秀文化艺术的基础上，踏踏实实走好自己的路，既不走逐步西化的歪路，也不走泥古不化的旧路。我们在传承中华古典诗词艺术中，扬弃其陈腐部分，吸收其精华成分，使中国诗歌流淌着中华文化的基因，发展和创新今天的新诗。

“不要人夸好颜色，只留清气满乾坤。”（元 · 王冕《墨梅》）在新形势下，新诗的创作要有文化自信，要更具有中华文化元素和气息，在传承中华民族优秀古典诗歌文化、学习民歌和借鉴外国诗歌中发展，在创新当代诗歌艺术中实现跨越。通过汲古润今，创作出更多具有家国情怀、情真意美、大众喜爱的诗篇，借以传承华夏文明的圣火，描绘出新天新地新时代。

完稿于 2024 年 3 月 26 日

诗与情

情，就是人们所说的包含喜怒哀乐的思想情感。在有阶级的社会里，它往往表现出不同的爱与憎。诗歌，如唐代大诗人白居易所说，是由于“情理动于内，随感遇而形于叹咏者”（《与元九书》）。所以我们说诗歌成之于情而又抒之以情。因而，诗歌应当比其他文艺作品更要以情动人，更要通过打动人的感情来起到教育和鼓舞作用。

有情方能有诗。诗歌的创作，总是由于社会生活激起了作者的爱憎，才迸发出带有强烈情感的诗。天安门诗歌运动中那诗的涛、歌的潮，就是这样涌现的。“创作总根于爱”。如果不是由于人们对周总理的无比深厚、无比真挚的爱，是不会有“万众一心由衷曲，愿将百死换一生”[1]这样令人心碎的呼唤，也不会有对“满腔热血为民洒，一身洁白玉无瑕”[2]的由衷的礼赞，当然更不能有成千上万情真辞切、朴素自然的诗歌。愤怒出诗人，也正是由于对“四人帮”强烈的憎恨，千百万人民群众在很短的时间内都成了诗人，发出了“驱妖邪，莫慈悲，要以刀枪对”[3]的怒吼。这些诗是爱与憎的结晶，是阶级感情的强烈迸发，是人民的“心底歌”，因而它们是“真正的诗”。所以我们说，诗歌作者只有在感情炽热，即大诗人郭沫若所谓的“冲动”时，方宜进入诗歌的创作。否则，即使硬作出来，它也不能活在人们的心中，因为没有感情，不动人的诗歌不是真正的诗，至少可以说它不算是好诗。

诗歌，是一种最便于直抒胸臆的文学样式。一首好的诗歌，应当抒发出强烈、饱满的情感，并以此去打动人们的心弦。恩格斯之所以赞赏宪章派工人爱德华·波·米德的诗歌——《蒸气王》，不但亲自把它译成德文，而且在《英国工人阶级状况》一书中加以引用，正是由于这首诗“正确地表达了工人中的普遍的情绪”。诗歌只有深刻地、正确地表达了思想感情（即情真意切），才能发挥它特有的艺术魅力，引起读者思想感情上强烈的反响，起到教育人民、鼓舞人民和打击敌人的作用，特别是有些抒情味道浓厚的诗歌，能够使人一唱三叹。为大家所熟知的贺敬之的《回延安》，由于抒发了强烈的对革命圣地延安的热爱之情，所以诗的一开头，那种澎湃、真挚、深厚的感情便一下子抓住了读者的心：“心儿呀，莫要这样厉害地跳，灰尘呀，莫把眼睛挡住了〞，“手抓黄土我不放，紧紧贴在心窝上”，“几回回梦里回延安，双手搂定宝塔山”。读到“千声万声呼唤你，——母亲延安就在这里”时，会让人感到诗人那抑制不住的热爱延安之情。这就是我们说的诗歌不能直言浅露，不能直着嗓子干喊，而应将丰富的感情与各种艺术手法有机地结合起来，使之凝练、含蓄，以达到“诗美”的境界。

古人云：“文章兴作，先动气。气生乎心，心发乎言。”动气即动情，情动而言形。情对于诗歌的确十分重要，在某种程度上可以说情就是诗，没有情也就失去了诗。当然，这种情感不是诗人心灵固有的，也不是文艺女神赐给的，它是丰富的社会生活撞击心扉而激起的音波，是不平常的生活实践搅起的思想上爱与憎的汹涌浪潮，只有当这强烈的音波、汹涌的浪潮冲破闸门和溢出堤坝，那才可能有佳诗的酿成。我们的诗歌作者只有深入到社会生活中去，才能汲取丰富的灵感，才能有助于我们减少那些无病呻吟之作，杜绝那些空泛的说教之辞，才能唱出人民心底的歌，写出时代的新诗篇。除此而外，难寻良方。这正如诗人和评论家何其芳所说：“好的诗，总是作者在生活中有感动才可能写出来，不应该没有创作冲动就硬去作诗。”[4]这是值得我们认真品味的。

今天中国现代新诗的创作和发展，应该更加重视和认识到“情”在诗歌中的重要性。特别是在人工智能时代到来的现在和将来，在AI也可以写诗的情况下，也许只有真情实感，才能证明真正的诗人和真正的诗歌了。

附注：

[1] [2] [3] 见《天安门诗抄》，人民文学出版社，1978。

[4] 见何其芳《谈写诗》，《新华日报》1940 年 1 月 20 日。

难忘的记忆（代跋）

辛丑年的春天，似乎来得格外早：草长莺飞了，百花送香了，娱乐场所开业了……我的心情也随着升温的天气，温暖而安好。但是这个牛年，注定是不平静的一年。妻子在医院刚要手术，3月21日下午，我又接到了同学传来的噩耗：我们中学时期的老师、河南师范大学教授、中国语文教育和文章学大师曾祥芹先生，因肺癌突发、医治无效，于郑州去世。我一下子惊呆了。前年五月中旬，与一众同学去看望先生时，他还身体康健、精神饱满，虽已八十三岁高龄，仍弹起钢琴，为大家助兴。没承想那次的合影，成了先生与大家最后的合照。虽说人有生老病死、天有阴晴雨雪，可叹世事难料、人生无常。逝者已逝，然有些记忆，是无法忘记的。

与先生初识于1971年。那时我初中毕业后，进入内黄县城关高中读书，语文老师和班主任即曾先生。第二年，城关高中并入只有一个体育场之隔的内黄县一中，曾先生仍然是我们的语文老师和班主任，直至1973年3月高中毕业。当时，先生已是这个豫北县城有名的“笔杆子”了，担任过《新内黄》报的主编。但是在那个讲成分、论阶级的年代，先生的人生并不得意。可他却是整天乐呵呵的，把精力都放在了教学和写文章上，白天在课堂上认真讲授知识，晚上伏在灯下努力备课、写文章，成了大家公认的、全县数一数二的语文教师。他对学生的请教，总是不厌其烦地耐心讲解。对学生们不理解的知识，他往往循循善诱、引导学生开阔视野，以掌握其要义。记得一次语文课上，讲到了“实事求是”这个词，同学们对它即科学地研究客观事物规律的含义，不甚理解。课间休息时，先生得知这个情况后，在接下来的课堂上，专门将这个固定词组拆分讲解。从语法到结构，从图像到释义，从出处到现实，深入浅出，一步步讲解，一层层剖析，使学生们理解了“实事”即客观存在的事物，“求”就是探索和寻求，“是”即内在联系及发展的规律，从而明白了这个成语的逻辑关系，加深了印象和理解，认识到了要按照事物的实际情况办事。想来，这个成语学且不易，行则更难。否则，伟人们就不会一再强调它了。先生渊博的知识、呕心沥血的教授、和蔼可亲的态度，使学生们非常喜欢听他讲的课，对他也更加敬重。也正是得益于先生的教学，我后来在上大学期间，学习语法也就不那么吃力了。

曾先生湖南人，出身望族，十八岁即从事语文教学，桃李满天下，教过无数班级，但是在教我们这一届时，应该说是他生活最狼狈的时期。三个子女还小，最大的才十岁左右，特别是夫人刘老师，常年体弱多病、甚至卧床不起，而先生的教学任务又重，所以他往往力不从心。那时，他的家和我们学生宿舍在一个小四合院里，东面是大门连着两边的墙，南面与西面几间房子住着学生，北面两三间房子就住着先生一家五口人，既是他休息的地方，又是他备课和写文章的地方。因此，当时经常看到先生下了课，不但要买菜做饭，还要照顾夫人和孩子，忙得不可开交，家里大一点的孩子就要干和煤泥、挑水等重活儿。我们几个班干部和同学们于心不忍，便经常帮他们做些力所能及的家务活儿。在干活儿的同时，有时同学们也请教一些学习上的问题，讨论对一些事情不同的看法。时间一长，再加上先生总是一副笑眯眯的样子，可亲可敬，所以师生之间相处得亦师亦友，如同家人。甚至有时难免忘记“师道尊严”，放肆地讨论一些问题。先生从来不批评说你错了，总是和颜悦色地一再重申自己的看法——哎、哎、你听我说……，哎、哎、哎，你听我跟你说……，直至把你说服。高中毕业考试那年，有一件事情令我十分的汗颜。当时，语文的毕业考试题是写一篇政论文。考试结果出来，我取得了年级最高分——96分。但同时也发现，还有一名同学和我的分数一样，即并列第一。我便不服输地要来这位同学的文章，匆匆看了看，觉得人家的文章报刊语言较多，不如我是用自己的想法和语言写出来的好。从小学开始，作文就是自己的强项，中学又受到先生重点培养，一路走来，自己的作文没少在课堂上被老师们点赞。现在出了个并列第一，就有些不服气。

当时年轻气傲和幼稚的我，便找到先生表达不满。先生给我讲解了文章的要义、吸收资料的必要等，使我认识到同学的文章论据珠联璧合、论证逻辑严密、论点无懈可击，确是一篇好文章。先生接着压低声音，认真地给我讲了谦虚使人进步、骄傲使人落后的道理，特别是他关于“越是有本事的人越谦虚谨慎、越低调”、“我们要夹起尾巴做人”的教诲，至今记忆犹新。其实，这又何尝不是先生自己的写照。他一生勤勤恳恳地授业，诲人不倦地育人，培养了一批又一批学生，在学术上也取得了巨大成就，但从来都是低调做人。这也许是学生们对他敬爱有加的原因。

还有一件遗憾的事儿，使我始终难忘。那是我高中毕业“上山下乡”后，1975年元月上旬，我和田氏良种繁育场的知青们干完农活儿，刚回到宿舍，收到了一封共青团河南省委宣传部写给我的信。原来，上年河南人民出版社与团省委共同征稿出版的诗集《广阔天地新一代》，已初步编好，但诗集的第一部分内容还不够。他们认为，“因你的诗写得很有基础，所以想让你写一首反映这方面内容的诗”，而且要求元月10日以前寄到。我深知这首诗歌的重要性，但是距离交稿的时间只有三四天了，除非自己手边有此类诗稿，否则真是赶不出来。情急之下便想找先生商量怎么办。第二天，骑车来到40多里外的县城，先生看了约稿信函后，一边鼓励我要“死马当活马医”，争取完成这个重要任务；一边把他的书桌清理干净，让我在那里写作。同时，还把孩子们都安排出去，不让他们影响我构思。他也计划下午下课后，与我一块儿“开夜车”。先生对于文章事业，从来都看得很重，甚至比穿衣吃饭都重要。他吃饭有辣椒即可，衣服不论新旧，然而会为写一个句子、一个标点符号，反复推敲，反复修改，直到完美。他自己是这样，对学生要求也是这样。晚上，在我拿出草稿的基础上，我们共同从主题到内容、从开头到结尾、从结构到激情、从诗句到字词，逐一讨论和修改，逐一斟酌和取舍。不觉已到了后半夜，先生困了就在书桌旁的床上睡一会儿，我困了就在椅子上眯一会儿，醒来又继续推敲、修改，直到天快亮时，才基本定下稿子。我俩就在那张床上，一个头朝北，一个头朝南，拥被和衣而卧。虽然屋里很冷，由于太疲乏，当我醒来时，已是艳阳高照。不知先生什么时候起的床，并已给我留好了早饭。又经过整理、誊写和完善，这篇标题为《上山下乡颂》的诗歌，终于在10日前寄出。当年11月诗歌集出版，12月收到团省委宣传部寄来的诗集后，我才发现没有收录这首诗歌，很遗憾！当时的通信联络工具，不像现在这么发达，乡下农场里的摇把电话机，是没有长途电话功能的，县内联系尚需总机、分机层层转接，县外联系就可想而知了。如需联系主要靠写信，从县里到郑州的信件，最少需要三天左右，从农场寄信时间就更长了。由于联系不畅，还是误了时间。这件事虽然很遗憾，但是先生对待写作的那种拼命精神，对待文章那种高度重视的态度，对待学生那种忘我的帮助，我是永远难忘的。也许在他的文章事业中，这件事微不足道，但是通过这一丝一毫可以看出，在他的心里道德文章大如天！

先生已驭鹤西去，然其教书、育人、写文章的功德，可以说是圆满的。他的道德文章，将永远留在学生和同仁们的心中。

——于 2021 年 5 月 5 日立夏